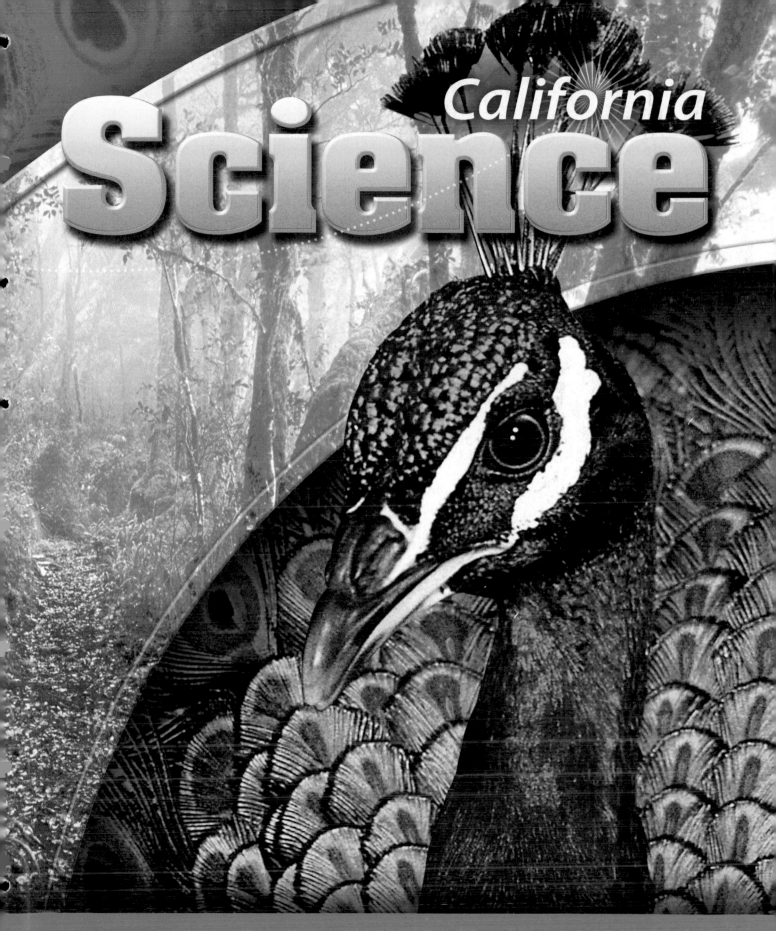

California Science

California

PEARSON

Scott
Foresman

Editorial Offices: Glenview, Illinois • Parsippany, New Jersey • New York, New York
Sales Offices: Boston, Massachusetts • Duluth, Georgia • Glenview, Illinois •
Coppell, Texas • Sacramento, California • Mesa, Arizona

Series Authors

Dr. Timothy Cooney
Professor of Earth Science and Science Education
University of Northern Iowa (UNI)
Cedar Falls, Iowa

Dr. Jim Cummins
Professor
Department of Curriculum, Teaching, and Learning
University of Toronto
Toronto, Canada

Dr. James Flood
Distinguished Professor of Literacy and Language
School of Teacher Education
San Diego State University
San Diego, California

Barbara Kay Foots, M.Ed.
Science Education Consultant
Houston, Texas

Dr. M. Jenice Goldston
Associate Professor of Science Education
Department of Elementary Education Programs
University of Alabama
Tuscaloosa, Alabama

Dr. Shirley Gholston Key
Associate Professor of Science Education
Instruction and Curriculum Leadership Department
College of Education
University of Memphis
Memphis, Tennessee

Dr. Diane Lapp
Distinguished Professor of Reading and Language Arts in Teacher Education
San Diego State University
San Diego, California

Sheryl A. Mercier
Classroom Teacher
Dunlap Elementary School
Dunlap, California

Karen L. Ostlund, Ph.D.
UTeach Specialist
College of Natural Sciences
The University of Texas at Austin
Austin, Texas

Dr. Nancy Romance
Professor of Science Education & Principal Investigator
NSF/IERI Science IDEAS Project
Charles E. Schmidt College of Science
Florida Atlantic University
Boca Raton, Florida

Dr. William Tate
Chair and Professor of Education and Applied Statistics
Department of Education
Washington University
St. Louis, Missouri

Dr. Kathryn C. Thornton
Former NASA Astronaut Professor
School of Engineering and Applied Science
University of Virginia
Charlottesville, Virginia

Dr. Leon Ukens
Professor Emeritus
Department of Physics, Astronomy, and Geosciences
Towson University
Towson, Maryland

Steve Weinberg
Consultant
Connecticut Center for Advanced Technology
East Hartford, Connecticut

ISBN: 0-328-18840-9

2 3 4 5 6 7 8 9 10 V057 15 14 13 12 11 10 09 08 07

Contributing Author

Dr. Michael P. Klentschy
Superintendent
El Centro Elementary School District
El Centro, California

Consulting Author

Dr. Olga Amaral
Chair, Division of Teacher Education
San Diego State University
Calexico, California

Science Content Consultants

Dr. Herbert Brunkhorst
Chair
Department of Science, Mathematics and Technology
College of Education
California State University, San Bernardino
San Bernardino, California

Dr. Karen Kolehmainen
Department of Physics
California State University, San Bernardino
San Bernardino, California

Dr. Stephen D. Lewis
Earth and Environmental Sciences
California State University, Fresno
Fresno, California

NASA Content Consultants

Adena Williams Loston, Ph.D.
Chief Education Officer
Office of the Chief Education Officer

Clifford W. Houston, Ph.D.
Deputy Chief Education Officer for Education Programs
Office of the Chief Education Officer

Frank C. Owens
Senior Policy Advisor
Office of the Chief Education Officer

Deborah Brown Biggs
Manager, Education Flight Projects Office
Space Operations Mission Directorate, Education Lead

Erika G. Vick
NASA Liaison to Pearson Scott Foresman
Education Flight Projects Office

William E. Anderson
Partnership Manager for Education
Aeronautics Research Mission Directorate

Anita Krishnamurthi
Program Planning Specialist
Space Science Education and Outreach Program

Bonnie J. McClain
Chief of Education
Exploration Systems Mission Directorate

Diane Clayton, Ph.D.
Program Scientist
Earth Science Education

Deborah Rivera
Strategic Alliances Manager
Office of Public Affairs
NASA Headquarters

Douglas D. Peterson
Public Affairs Office, Astronaut Office
Office of Public Affairs
NASA Johnson Space Center

Nicole Cloutier
Public Affairs Office, Astronaut Office
Office of Public Affairs
NASA Johnson Space Center

iii

Reviewers

California

Science

How does electricity behave, and how is it useful?

Chapter 2 • Magnetism

What is magnetism, and how is it useful?

How do living things interact in an ecosystem?

How can ecosystems be described?

Chapter 5 • Interactions in Ecosystems

How do living things survive in an ecosystem?

CALIFORNIA Unit C Earth Sciences

How are rocks and minerals formed?

Chapter 6 • Minerals and Rocks

Chapter 7 • Our Changing Earth

How is Earth's surface shaped and reshaped?

Science Process Skills

Observe

A scientist investigating Muir Woods National Monument observes many things. You use your senses when you find out about other objects, events, or living things.

Classify

Scientists classify living things in Muir Woods according to their characteristics. When you classify, you arrange or sort objects, events, or living things.

Estimate and Measure

Scientists might estimate the size of a coast redwood tree in Muir Woods. When they estimate, they tell what they think the object's size, mass, or temperature will measure. They then measure these factors in units.

Scientists use process skills when they investigate places or events. You will use these skills when you do the activities in this book. Which process skills might scientists use when they investigate animals and plants such as those found in Muir Woods National Monument near San Francisco?

Infer

During an investigation, scientists use what they already know to infer what they think is happening.

Predict

Before they go into Muir Woods, scientists tell what they think they will find.

Make and Use Models

Scientists might make and use models, to help plan what they want to study during an investigation.

Science Process Skills

Investigate and Experiment
As the scientists explore Muir Woods, they investigate and experiment to test a hypothesis.

Form Questions and Hypotheses
Think of a statement that you can test to solve a problem or answer a question about the animals and plants you see in Muir Woods.

Identify and Control Variables
As scientists perform an experiment, they identify and control the variables. They must test only one thing at a time.

If you were a scientist, you might learn more about Muir Woods. What questions might you have about the living and nonliving things you see? How would you use process skills in your investigation?

Collect Data
Scientists collect data from their observations in Muir Woods. They organize the data into charts or tables.

Interpret Data
Scientists use the information they collected to solve problems and answer questions.

Communicate
Scientists use words, pictures, charts, and graphs to share information about their investigation.

Using Scientific Methods for Science Inquiry

Scientists use scientific methods as they work. Scientific methods are organized ways to answer questions and solve problems. Scientific methods include the steps shown here. Scientists might not use all the steps. They might not use the steps in this order. You will use scientific methods when you do the **Full Inquiry** activity at the end of each unit. You also will use scientific methods when you do Science Fair Projects.

Ask a question.
You might have a question about something you observe.

What material is best for keeping heat in water?

State your hypothesis.
A hypothesis is a possible answer to your question.

If I wrap the jar in fake fur, then the water will stay warmer longer.

Identify and control variables.
Variables are things that can change. For a fair test, you can can change just one variable. All other variables must be the same.

Test other materials. Put the same amount of warm water in other jars that are the same type, size, and shape.

Test your hypothesis.

Make a plan to test your hypothesis. Collect materials and tools. Then follow your plan.

Collect and record your data.

Keep good records of what you do and find out. Use tables and pictures to help.

Interpret your data.

Organize your notes and records to make them clear. Make diagrams, charts, or graphs to help.

State your conclusion.

Your conclusion is a decision you make based on your data. Communicate what you found out. Tell whether or not your data supported your hypothesis.

Fake fur did the best job of keeping the water warm.

Go further.

Use what you learn. Think of new questions to test or better ways to do a test.

Ask a Question

State Your Hypothesis

Identify and Control Variables

Test Your Hypothesis

Collect and Record Your Data

Interpret Your Data

State Your Conclusion

Go Further

Science Tools

Scientists use many different kinds of tools. Tools can make objects appear larger. They can help you measure volume, temperature, length, distance, and mass. Tools can help you figure out amounts and analyze your data.

A **graduated cylinder** or **graduated cup** can be used to measure volume, or the amount of space an object takes up.

A **spring scale** measures the force of gravity on an object. It is a type of force meter.

Balances are used to measure mass.

You use **metric rulers** or **metersticks** to measure length and distance.

A **microscope** uses several lenses to make small objects appear much larger. You are able to see more detail.

You can protect your eyes by wearing safety goggles.

You use a **thermometer** to measure temperature. Many thermometers have both Fahrenheit and Celsius scales. Scientists usually use only the Celsius scale.

A **magnifying lens** or hand lens makes objects appear larger and shows more detail than you could see with just your eyes. A hand lens doesn't enlarge things as much as a microscope does, but it is easier to take with you.

You can use a **compass** to detect magnetic effects, such as Earth's magnetic field. A compass needle will detect and react to nearby magnets.

Safety

Safety in the Classroom

Scientists know they must work safely when doing experiments. You need to be careful when doing science activities too. Follow these safety rules:

- Read the activity carefully before you start.
- Listen to the teacher's instructions. Ask questions about things you do not understand.
- Wear safety goggles when needed.
- Keep your work area neat and clean.
- Clean up spills right away.
- Never taste or smell substances unless directed to do so by your teacher.
- Handle sharp items and other equipment carefully.
- Use chemicals carefully.
- Help keep plants and animals that you use safe.
- Tell your teacher if you see something that looks unsafe or if there is an accident.
- Put materials away when you finish.
- Dispose of chemicals properly.
- Wash your hands well when you are finished.

Safety at Home

Safety Tips

- Put toys, clothing, shoes, and books away. Do not leave anything lying on the floor.
- Do not play with sharp objects such as knives.
- Wash your hands with soap and warm water before you eat.
- Clean up all spills right away.
- Turn on a light before walking into a dark room.
- Do not run indoors.
- Do not jump down stairs.

Safety

Science Safety Tips

- Think about safety tips that you follow in your classroom.
- Do science activities only when an adult is with you.
- Never taste, touch, or smell anything unless your teacher or someone in your family tells you it is okay.

Fire Safety Tips

- Never use matches or lighters.
- Never use the stove or oven without the help of an adult.
- Get out quickly if a building you are in is on fire.
- Stop, drop, and roll if your clothing catches on fire. Do not run.
- Know two ways to get out of your home.
- Practice fire escape routes with your family.

Stop

Drop

Roll

Electrical Safety Tips

- Do not touch electrical outlets. When they are not in use, cover them with safety caps.
- Always unplug appliances by pulling on the plug instead of the cord. Pulling on the cord can damage the wires.
- A cord that has damaged insulation should be replaced immediately.
- Never touch a power line with your body or any object. Stay far away from downed power lines. If you see one, call 911.
- Never touch an electrical appliance, switch, cord, plug, or outlet if you or the appliance is touching water.
- Do not use cord-operated radios or other electrical appliances near a bathtub, pool, or lake. Use battery-operated devices instead.

Earthquake Tips

- Help your family make an earthquake kit. Put water, food, a flashlight, and a portable radio in your kit.
- Make a plan with an adult about what to do if there is an earthquake.
- Get under or lie next to a heavy table, desk, or piece of furniture.
- Stay away from glass doors and windows.

Metric and Customary Measurement

The metric system is the measurement system most commonly used in science. Metric units are sometimes called SI units. SI stands for International System. It is called that because these units are used around the world.

These prefixes are used in the metric system:

kilo- means *thousand*

1 kilometer equals 1,000 meters

milli- means *one-thousandth*
1,000 millimeters equals 1 meter or 1 millimeter = 0.001 meter

centi- means *one-hundredth*
100 centimeters equals 1 meter or 1 centimeter = 0.01 meter

Length and Distance
One meter is longer than 1 yard.

1 yard

1 meter

Mass
One kilogram is greater than 1 pound.

1 pound

1 kilogram

Volume
One liter is greater than 4 cups.

1 liter

1 cup

Temperature
Water freezes at 0°C or 32°F.
Water boils at 100°C or 212°F.

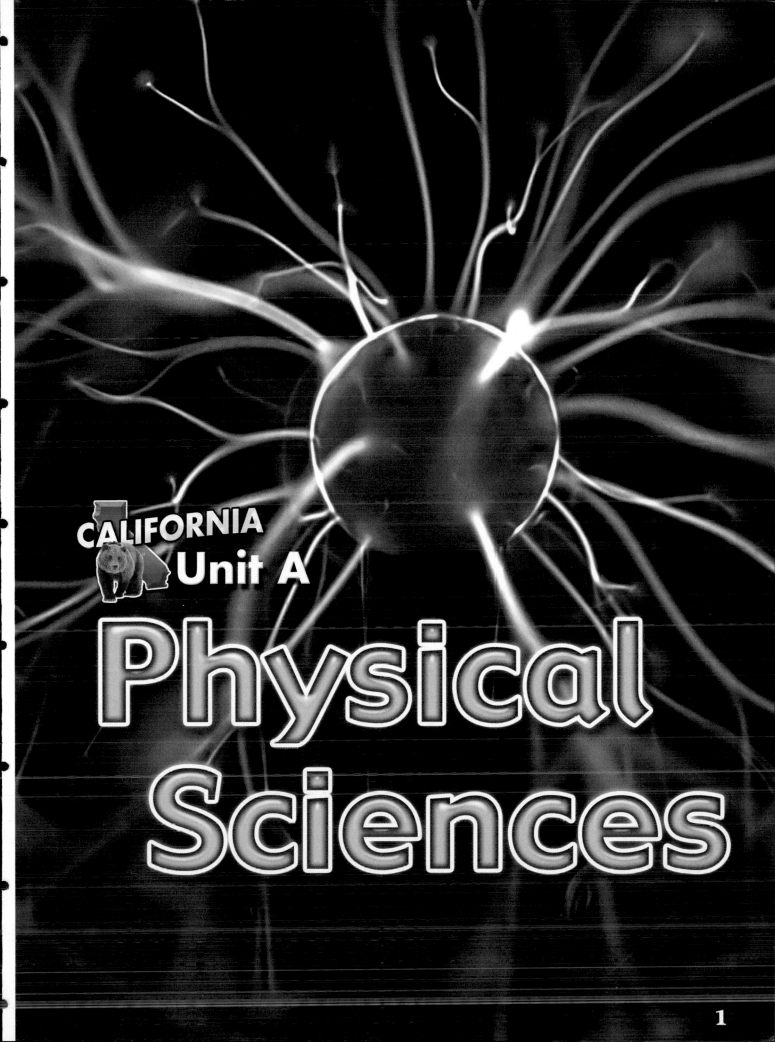

CALIFORNIA
Unit A

Physical Sciences

Shasta Dam and Power Plant

Redding, California

You can see how water is used to make electricity if you visit Shasta Dam and Power Plant at Shasta Lake, north of Redding. It's the second-largest dam in the United States. The waterfall it creates is the largest such waterfall in the world. Another result of the dam is Shasta Lake, California's largest reservoir made by people.

Many people visit Shasta Lake for recreation, but the real action happens beneath the dam. Some of the water from Shasta Lake flows through pipes called penstocks at the base of the dam. This water spins five huge electrical generators. Each generator is more than 18 meters tall. Each produces electricity as it spins. Wires carry this electricity to a switchyard and then to places throughout California.

Shasta
Dam and
Power Plant

Find Out More

Find out more about how electricity is generated with flowing water. Choose a project to show what you learned.

- Make a booklet for people visiting Shasta Dam and Power Plant or another dam in California.

- Draw a diagram showing how water passes through a dam and spins the turbines that generate electricity. Write a sentence that explains what happens at each step in your diagram.

Chapter 1

Electricity

CALIFORNIA Standards Preview

4PS1.0 Electricity and magnetism are related effects that have many useful applications in everyday life. As a basis for understanding this concept:

4PS1.a Students know to design and build simple series and parallel circuits by using components such as wires, batteries, and bulbs.

4PS1.e Students know electrically charged objects attract or repel each other.

4PS1.g Students know how electrical energy can be converted into heat, light, and motion.

4IE6.0 Scientific progress is made by asking meaningful questions and conducting careful investigations. As a basis for understanding this concept and addressing the content in the other three strands, students should develop their own questions and perform investigations. (Also **4IE6.a**, **4IE6.c**, **4IE6.f**)

Standards Focus Questions

- How do charged objects behave?

- How do electric charges move?

- What are parallel circuits?

How does electricity behave, and how is it useful?

static electricity

electric charge

series circuit

4

Chapter 1 Vocabulary

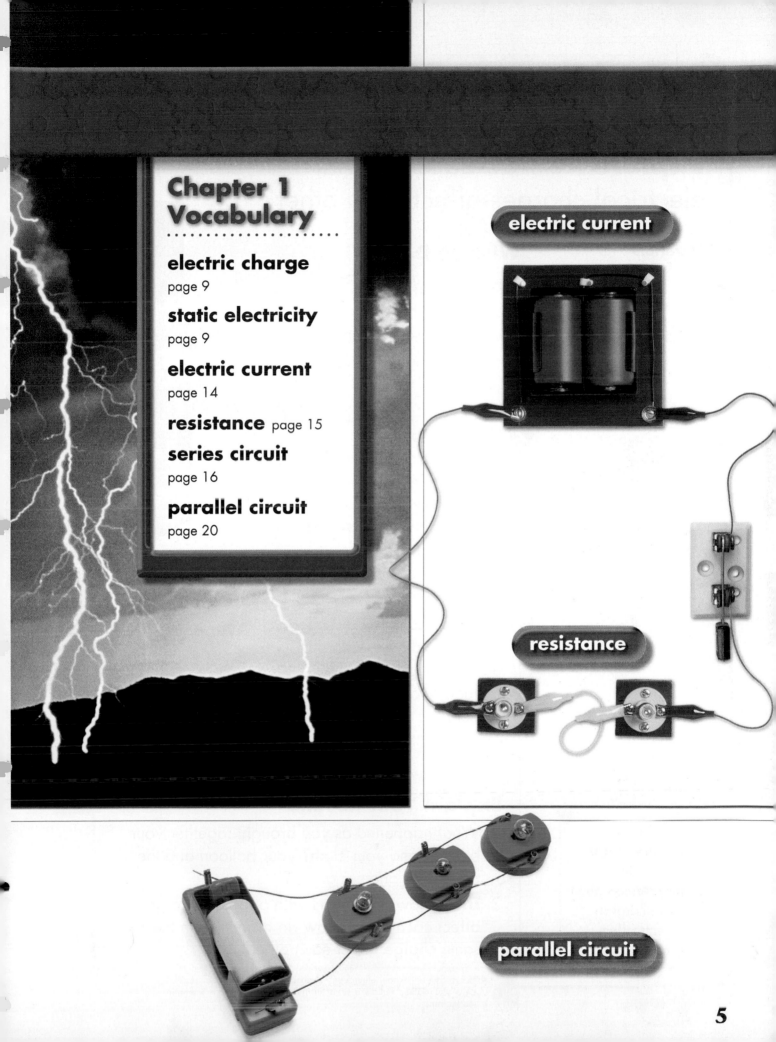

electric current

resistance

parallel circuit

Explore How do balloons with electrical charges affect each other?

Materials

safety goggles

balloon with thread

wool cloth

What to Do

1 Rub *ALL* parts of a balloon with a wool cloth for about 1 minute.

The balloon has a negative charge.

The cloth has a positive charge.

2 Hold your balloon by the thread. Hold your cloth about an arm's length away. Slowly bring them closer together. **Observe.**

3 Rub *ALL* parts of your balloon again. Hold it by its thread. Slowly bring it near the balloon of another group. Observe.

Both balloons have a negative charge.

Explain Your Results

1. What happened as you brought together your balloon and your cloth? your balloon and the balloon of another group?

2. **Infer** How do objects with opposite charges affect each other? How do objects with the same charge affect each other?

4PS1.e Students know electrically charged objects attract or repel each other. **4IE6.f** Follow a set of written instructions for a scientific investigation.

How to Read Science

Cause and Effect

Learning to find **causes and effects** can help you understand what you read. A cause may have more than one effect. An effect may have more than one cause. Words such as *because, so,* and *as a result* may signal cause and effect. Sometimes you can **infer** cause and effect based on what you've observed.

Look for causes and effects in the advertisement below.

Magazine Advertisement

Feeling positively negative about clinging clothes?
Does static electricity rub you the wrong way?
Take charge! Try **ELECTRO-NOT!**

This new spray tames static electricity. Spray it on socks before putting them in the dryer so they don't stick to your shirts. Your hair will no longer stand up when you remove your winter hat. Because of our anti-cling technology, ELECTRO-NOT neutralizes the charges that build up on your clothing. Let the sparks fly in your campfire, not on your clothes. Buy ELECTRO-NOT today. Your socks will be glad you did!

Apply It!
Use the **causes and effects** and **inferences** you can make from the advertisement to complete a graphic organizer.

You Are There!

ZZZAPP! A jagged bolt of lightning slashes and flashes through the sky. Less than a second later, it's gone. But then more and more brilliant bolts appear, briefly connecting the clouds to the ground. Like snowflakes and grains of sand, each bolt is unique. BOOOOM!! The sound of thunder startles you. You are glad that you are indoors, watching this dazzling display through a window. What causes this beautiful, super-charged sight that can pack a deadly wallop?

Standards Focus 4PS1.0 Electricity and magnetism are related effects that have many useful applications in everyday life. As a basis for understanding this concept:

4PS1.e Students know electrically charged objects attract or repel each other.

4IE6.0 Scientific progress is made by asking meaningful questions and conducting careful investigations. As a basis for understanding this concept and addressing the content in the other three strands, students should develop their own questions and perform investigations. Students will:

4IE6.a Differentiate observation from inference (interpretation) and know scientists' explanations come partly from what they observe and partly from how they interpret their observations.

DIGITAL

How do charged objects behave?

The build-up of electrical charges causes static electricity. Unlike charges attract and like charges repel each other.

Electric Charges

Did you know that big, bright lightning bolts are caused by particles much too small to see? Strange, isn't it? Matter is made of tiny particles called atoms. Atoms are made of even smaller particles. Some of these particles have electric charge.

An **electric charge** is a property of some parts of matter that is described as positive or negative. If matter has as many positive as negative charges, the charges balance. The matter has no charge. It is *neutral*. Matter with more positive than negative charges is positively charged. Objects with unlike charges are pulled toward, or *attract*, each other. Objects with like charges are pushed away from, or *repel*, each other.

Static Electricity

Electrons are the negatively charged particles in atoms. When objects are near each other, electrons can move from one object to another. The object that gains electrons becomes negatively charged. The object that loses electrons becomes positively charged. The built-up charges are **static electricity.**

So what does static electricity have to do with lightning? Ice and water droplets inside clouds rub against each other. Electrons move. Positive charges build up near the top of clouds, and negative charges build up near the bottom. In time, the static electrical energy is released. The energy heats up the air, making it glow as lightning!

1. **✓Checkpoint** What happens when two objects with like charges are near each other?

2. An object has more negative than positive charges. How is the object charged?

How Charged Objects Behave

You've just read that unlike charges attract each other and that like charges repel each other. You can see this happen with just a balloon and your hair! Look at the girl in the photo. You can see her long, fine hair is pulling toward the balloon. You could infer that her hair and the balloon have unlike charges. How could that happen?

If you rub a balloon on your hair, electrons move from your hair to the balloon. The added electrons make the balloon negatively charged. And, after losing electrons, the strands of hair become positively charged. If you hold the balloon near your head, the unlike charges attract each other. Your hair moves toward the balloon.

Look at the photo again. Did you notice that the strands of hair are standing apart from each other? Remember that objects with a like charge repel each other. Each strand of hair has a positive charge. The strands repel each other. They move as far away from each other as they can.

Electrons on the Move

The same thing happens when you wear a wool cap. As the wool rubs against your hair, electrons move from your hair to the cap. The cap becomes negatively charged and your hair becomes positively charged. When you take off the cap—WHOA! All the hairs stand up and move as far apart as possible. Their positive charges repel each other.

10

Scuff, Scuff, Zap!

Have you ever shocked yourself on a metal doorknob? Electric charges caused the jolt of energy you felt. When you scuff your feet along a carpet, you pick up extra electrons. You become negatively charged. When you touch the metal doorknob, electrons travel from you to the doorknob. You might even see the spark caused by the static electricity. The spark is like a miniature flash of lightning!

1. ✓**Checkpoint** Why does your hair move toward a balloon after you rub the balloon on your head?

2. **Cause and Effect** What causes your body to build up a charge when you scuff your feet on a carpet?

11

Charging a Neutral Object

Suppose that you rub a balloon with a piece of silk. The balloon becomes negatively charged. Then you hold the balloon next to a pile of small pieces of paper. The picture shows what happens next. The pieces of paper move toward the balloon! But the paper was neutral. The pieces had no charge. Why are they attracted to the balloon?

Charged Objects' Effect on Neutral Objects

A neutral object contains particles that have positive charge and particles that have negative charge. The negatively charged balloon pushes away the negatively charged particles in the pieces of paper. The top of each piece—the side closest to the balloon—now has a positive charge. Because the paper is lightweight, the force between unlike charges is strong enough to pull the pieces to the balloon.

The pull between a charged object and a neutral object can be very strong. You can demonstrate this attraction. Rub a balloon on your hair or on a piece of wool and then hold the balloon next to a wall. The balloon clings to the wall! The extra negative charge on the balloon attracts the positively charged particles at the surface of the wall. The same thing happens when a balloon clings to your clothing.

The balloon will not cling forever. Over time, it loses its negative charge. It is neutral again. It no longer has the negative charge that attracted the positive particles in the wall or clothing. It falls to the floor.

Rub a balloon with plastic wrap. Then see if a sock will stick to it!

The balloon has a negative charge. It pushes away negative charges in the paper. The tops of the pieces of paper get a positive charge and are pulled toward the balloon.

The Force Between Charged Objects

The force between the charges pulls unlike charges together and pushes like charges apart. This force is strongest when the charged objects are close together. It weakens as the distance between the objects increases. This is why a charged balloon attracts your hair when it is close to your head but not when it is far away.

You can use balloons to feel the strength of the attracting or repelling force. If you rub two balloons on your hair or on a wool sock, you give each balloon a negative charge. You will see the balloons repelling each other when you bring them close together. You will feel the force pushing them apart. If you give one balloon a positive charge and another a negative charge, you will feel them pull toward each other.

These balloons have the same charge. They repel each other.

These balloons have opposite charges. They attract each other.

✓ Lesson Review

1. What effect will a negatively charged object have on a neutral object?

2. What effect will an object with a negative charge have on a second object that also has a negative charge?

3. **Writing in Science Narrative** Write a story that tells a curious first grader about static electricity. Include at least two events that show how unlike charges attract and like charges repel.

13

Lesson 2

How do electric charges move?

Electricity can travel through a circuit, or loop of wire. Batteries can cause electricity to flow. Switches can turn the flow on or off. Other devices change electric current into other forms of energy.

Charges in Motion

You flip the light switch on the wall and a light bulb across the room glows. How did the electricity get to the bulb? Electric charges in motion are called **electric current.** If the direction and flow of current are controlled, the path that the current follows is called an *electrical circuit.*

Energy Source
The energy source for this circuit is a pair of batteries. The batteries cause the electric charges to flow.

Wires
Copper wires and metal clips connect the parts of the circuit. They complete the path through which the electric charges flow.

Open Switch
The switch is open, so the circuit is broken. The flow of current is interrupted.

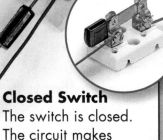

Closed Switch
The switch is closed. The circuit makes a complete loop. Electric current flows without interruption.

For current to flow, an electrical circuit must complete a loop. The current cannot flow if the loop has any breaks. A circuit that makes a loop is a *closed circuit.* An *open circuit* has at least one break. Follow the path of the closed circuit on these pages to see the parts of an electrical circuit.

Standards Focus 4PS1.0 Electricity and magnetism are related effects that have many useful applications in everyday life. As a basis for understanding this concept:
4PS1.a Students know how to design and build simple series and parallel circuits by using components such as wires, batteries, and bulbs.
4PS1.g Students know how electrical energy can be converted into heat, light, and motion.

Conductors, Resistors, and Insulators

The current flows through parts of the loop that are conductors. A *conductor* is a material that allows electricity to flow easily. The switches, wires, and clips are conductors. Many conductors are made of metal.

Most circuits also have at least one resistor. A *resistor* is a material that resists the flow of electric current. **Resistance** means that the material does not allow electric current to flow through easily. Even good conductors have a little resistance. Resistors transform electrical energy into light, heat, and other types of energy.

Resistor
The thin coiled wire inside the light bulb is a resistor. The wire's resistance causes moving electric charges to heat the wire. The wire gives off heat and light.

Insulators prevent the current from flowing. An *insulator* is a material that has so much resistance that it stops the current. The plastic coating on wires is an insulator. What other insulators can you name?

Glass insulators on power lines stop electric charges. The charges are not able to move through the support poles to the ground.

1. **√ Checkpoint** What is the role of a battery in a circuit?

2. **Cause and Effect** Why is an electrical circuit made of materials that are conductors?

keyword:
electric current
code.
gr4p14

Series Circuits

You have read that electricity can flow only through a closed circuit. The pictures on these pages show one type of circuit, called a series circuit. In a **series circuit**, electric charge can flow in only one circular path. Any break in the path stops the current from flowing.

Batteries provide the energy to move electric charges through some circuits. The lights shown at the left make a circuit, too, but they have a different power source. An electrical outlet connects the string of lights to a power plant through long-distance wires.

This string of lights is a series circuit. No bulbs light because one bulb is burnt out.

If this switch were open, no current could flow. When the switch is closed, the circuit is closed too. Current flows through the loop.

When the circuit is closed, the batteries provide the energy for the electric charges to start flowing through the loop. The wires conduct the charges through the closed switch to the resistors and then back to the batteries. The resistors change some of the energy into other forms of energy.

The electrical energy is shared among all the resistors in the circuit. If a circuit has two identical light bulbs, they will burn with the same brightness. However, one resistor burning out breaks the circuit, just as opening the switch does. The other resistors won't receive any current, so they won't light.

Series circuits are not used much anymore—even for strings of lights. Buildings rarely have series circuits. Appliances and other things that run on electrical energy need different amounts of current. Also, if one of them is turned off or broken, none of the other devices on the circuit will work.

1. ✔ **Checkpoint** In a series circuit with three tiny light bulbs, what will happen if one of the bulbs is removed from its socket?

2. **Cause and Effect** A third identical light bulb is wired into the series circuit on this page. What effect does this have?

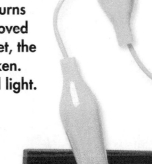

These bulbs are wired in a series circuit. If one bulb burns out or is removed from its socket, the circuit is broken. No bulbs will light.

A series circuit can have more than one resistor. Resistors transform electrical energy into other forms of energy. These light bulbs transform electrical energy into light and heat energy.

Energy Changing Form

The resistors in the circuit on pages 16 and 17 are light bulbs. Like most other resistors, light bulbs convert electrical energy into other forms that people can use. Resistors commonly convert electrical energy into heat, light, or motion.

Energy is never lost, but it can change form. When current passes through a resistor, some energy flows on to the rest of the circuit. Much of the energy changes into another form. Often it changes into heat. This is the reason that electrical wires sometimes become hot.

If resistance is strong enough, some of the energy can change into light. The part of a light bulb with the highest resistance is the filament. The filament is a very thin coiled wire that can get very hot without melting. Most of the energy that passes through the filament is transformed into heat. The filament gets so hot that it glows, also giving off light.

This light bulb filament has been enlarged so that you can easily see the thin wire coils.

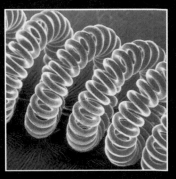

These light bulbs are resistors that convert electricity into light and heat. When lit, they quickly become too hot to touch.

Producing Heat and Light

Electricity powers many devices and appliances that you use every day. Toasters, televisions, computers, light bulbs, and many stoves all need electricity. Some of them are designed to produce light, although they always produce heat too. Others are designed to produce heat but may also produce light. Still others are designed to produce both heat and light. Look at the pictures on the right. Each shows an object that converts electricity into heat and light.

You may not be able to see the circuits that power a stove or a toaster, but you can see how energy changes forms in a simple circuit. The circuit shown here uses just a flashlight bulb and its holder, two pieces of wire, and a battery.

The bulb lights when the circuit is closed, so you can see that electrical energy is converted into light. You can't see the heat energy, but you can measure it with a thermometer. If you place the thermometer on the bulb, you can measure the change in temperature after the electrical energy starts flowing. When the temperature rises, you can conclude that electrical energy is also changed into heat.

The main purpose of a porch light is to convert electrical energy into light.

Electricity in heat lamps changes to heat and also to light. This meerkat is basking in the warmth from the heat lamp.

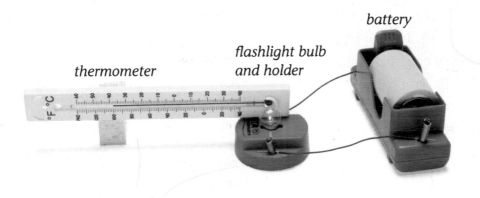

thermometer

flashlight bulb and holder

battery

When the current is on, resistance causes the electric stove burner to heat and give off orange light.

✓ Lesson Review

1. List three appliances that convert electrical energy into another form of energy. Identify the form or forms of energy each produces.

2. What part of a circuit converts electrical energy into other forms of energy?

3. **Cause and Effect** What causes a light bulb in a circuit to become hot and give off light?

Lesson 3

What are parallel circuits?

Parallel circuits are circuits that have more than one branch. The current can be switched off in one branch and still flow through the other branches.

Parallel Circuits

Suppose that you are hanging a string of lights for a party. Suddenly one bulb burns out. At first you worry that you'll have to replace the whole string. But then you see that the other bulbs are still lit. You know that this couldn't happen in a series circuit. Why didn't all of the lights go out?

The lights must be connected in a parallel circuit. A **parallel circuit** has two or more paths through which electric charges may flow. The main path or loop leaves from and returns to the power source. Smaller loops branch off from the main loop and then connect back to it. Electric charges can flow through any of the pathways on the circuit. If the circuit in one of the loops is broken, the current will still flow through all of the other loops.

Battery
Two batteries provide the power for the circuit.

Parallel Circuit
Start at the power source, and trace the circuit with your index finger. Follow each possible pathway that makes a complete loop. Name each part as you go.

1. ✓**Checkpoint** Describe a parallel circuit.

2. List two possible reasons that none of the bulbs in a parallel circuit is lit.

Look for Active Art animations at www.pearsonsuccessnet.com

Standards Focus 4PS1.0 Electricity and magnetism are related effects that have many useful applications in everyday life. As a basis for understanding this concept:
4PS1.a Students know how to design and build simple series and parallel circuits by using components such as wires, batteries, and bulbs.
4PS1.g Students know how electrical energy can be converted into heat, light, and motion.

Switch
The switch is closed. Charges can flow through the circuit.

Branch Point
At this branch point, the current divides. Part of the current travels through each branch.

If both bulbs have the same resistance, the amount of current flowing through them is also the same.

If the bulbs have different resistances, more current will flow through the bulb with less resistance.

Branch Point
At this branch point, the currents flowing through the branches join. All of the current returns to the battery through the same wire.

Series and Parallel Circuits

Your home has parallel circuits. So does your school. Why are parallel circuits used instead of series circuits? After all, a series circuit is simpler than a parallel circuit. It takes only one loop to make a series circuit.

The problem with series circuits is that if one resistor on the circuit is removed or burns out, all of the other resistors stop working too. If all of the lights in your house were connected in a series circuit, you could never turn off just one light! If you turned off one light, all of the lights would shut off.

A parallel circuit, on the other hand, has more than one possible loop. The circuit branches into different paths. If one path is broken, the others still work. If lights are connected in a parallel circuit, you can turn each light off or on without affecting the others. This makes parallel circuits more practical than series circuits in homes, schools, and other buildings.

This parallel circuit has three different paths for current. Trace each path from the battery, through a light bulb, and back to the battery.

One bulb is burnt out, opening that branch. The other two branches are still complete loops. Those bulbs stay lit.

In a parallel circuit, a missing or burnt bulb does not cause the others to go out. They stay lit.

Please Keep the Lights On

Think about the series lights you saw at the side of page 16. When one bulb burned out, all of the others went out too. The lights at the side of this page are in a parallel circuit. One bulb is burned out. But because this is a parallel circuit, the other bulbs stay lit.

Parallel circuits have another advantage. Appliances use different amounts of electricity. A radio or a clock uses only a small amount of current. A space heater, iron, or toaster uses much more current. Each branch of a parallel circuit takes only as much current as the resistors on that branch need. In a series circuit, the current is equal in all the resistors.

1. **Checkpoint** How are parallel circuits different from series circuits?

2. **Writing in Science Descriptive** Describe the path of electrical current through the parallel circuit shown on pages 22 and 23. Explain the purpose of each part of the circuit.

Electrical Safety

You have been learning some ways people make electric current useful. Electric current can also be very dangerous. It must be handled safely to prevent injury.

Electric charges always flow through the path with least resistance. A *short circuit* occurs when current follows a path other than the path meant for its flow. Short circuits often happen when a frayed or damaged wire touches a good conductor, such as metal or water. Salt water is a very good conductor. The fluids in your body are slightly salty, so you should never touch a bare wire!

Electrical Safety: Avoid These Shocking Hazards

1. Do not touch electrical outlets. When they are not in use, cover them with safety caps.
2. Always unplug appliances by pulling on the plug instead of the cord. Pulling on the cord can damage the wires.
3. Cords that have damaged insulation should be replaced.
4. Never touch a power line with your body or any object. Stay far away from downed power lines. If you see one, call 911.
5. Never touch an electrical appliance, switch, cord, plug, or outlet if you or the appliance is touching water.
6. Do not use cord-operated radios or other electrical appliances near a bathtub, pool, or lake. Use battery-operated devices instead.

Equipment or appliances that use large amounts of electricity need heavy-duty extension cords.

Some electrical circuits have fuses. If too much current flows, a thin metal strip in the fuse melts. This breaks the circuit and prevents damage that too much current might cause. After the strip melts, the fuse must be replaced. Which fuse do you think needs to be replaced?

An extension cord should be at least as thick as the appliance cord to which it connects. Thinner wires have greater resistance. Using too thin an extension cord is a fire hazard.

A circuit breaker is a switch. If too much current flows, the circuit breaker "trips" and the switch shuts off the circuit. The switch must be reset before the circuit will work again. If a circuit breaker trips, too many devices on that circuit are being used at the same time.

Have you ever seen a plug with three prongs? The round, third prong is not always part of the circuit. If too much current flows to electrical equipment, the third prong returns the extra current to the ground. The ground can absorb it safely.

✓ Lesson Review

1. Why is it important for wires in a circuit to be insulated?

2. How do circuit breakers and fuses limit the flow of current?

3. ✏ **Writing in Science**
   Descriptive Suppose that you turn on an appliance and all of the lights in the room go out. Write a plan describing steps that an adult could take to fix the problem.

Plastic or rubber insulation usually covers copper electrical wires. The insulation prevents your body from directly touching the wire.

Using Numbers to Represent Electrical Charges

Positive and negative numbers are often used in science. Numbers greater than zero are positive, and numbers less than zero are negative. Positive numbers can be written without a sign. So "positive five" can be written as +5 or 5. You have worked with positive and negative temperatures. You can also use positive and negative numbers to represent electrical charges.

When a neutral material loses particles with negative charges (electrons), it has a positive charge. An opposite charge makes it neutral again. If the charge is +5, a charge of –5 will make it neutral again.

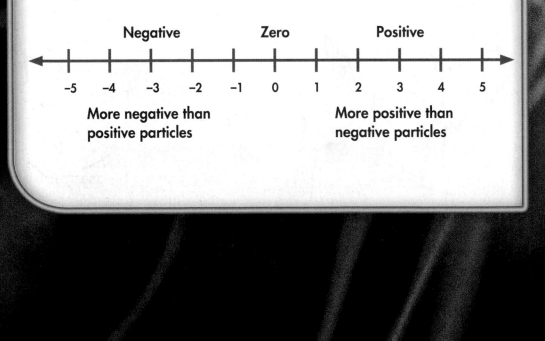

Negative					Zero				Positive	
-5	-4	-3	-2	-1	0	1	2	3	4	5

More negative than positive particles

More positive than negative particles

Answer these questions. Use a number line to help.

1. If a material has a charge of +4, what charge would make it neutral?
   A. +2
   B. −2
   C. +4
   D. −4

2. If a neutral balloon gains 3 negative charges (electrons) and then loses 3 negative charges (electrons), what will its charge be?
   A. +3
   B. −3
   C. 0
   D. +6

3. If a balloon with a negative charge and a balloon with a positive charge are held up by strings next to each other, what will happen?
   A. They will move toward each other.
   B. They will move apart.
   C. Nothing will happen.
   D. They will both fall to the floor.

Lab zone Take-Home Activity

Design an experiment in which you try to get charged balloons to stick to objects in your home, such as the refrigerator, a door, and so on. Time how long the balloon sticks to each (if it sticks at all). Make a table or graph to show your results. Try this experiment in different kinds of weather.

Investigate How are series and parallel circuits different?

Wear safety goggles.

Be careful!

Materials

safety goggles

battery and battery holder

2 flashlight bulbs and holders

4 pieces of wire

What to Do

1 Make a series circuit. Connect all parts. Record what happens to the light bulbs.

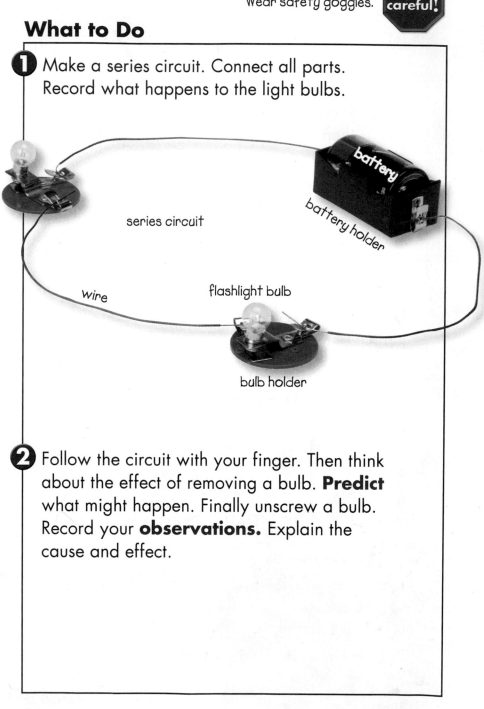

battery
battery holder

series circuit

wire

flashlight bulb

bulb holder

2 Follow the circuit with your finger. Then think about the effect of removing a bulb. **Predict** what might happen. Finally unscrew a bulb. Record your **observations.** Explain the cause and effect.

Process Skills

You can use cause-and-effect relationships to help make good **predictions.**

4PS1.a Students know how to design and build simple series and parallel circuits by using components such as wires, batteries, and bulbs. **4IE6.c** Formulate and justify predictions based on cause-and-effect relationships. (Also **4IE6.f**)

3 Make a parallel circuit. Connect all parts. Record what happens to the light bulbs.

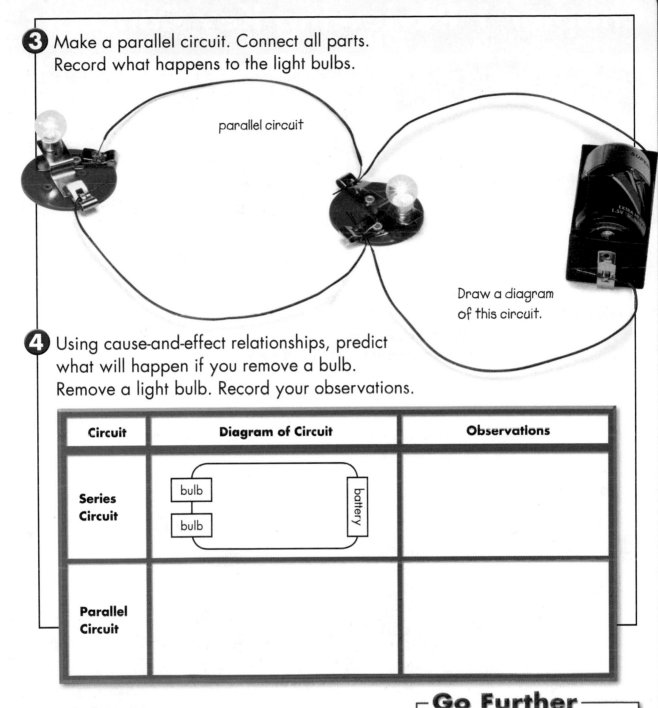

parallel circuit

Draw a diagram of this circuit.

4 Using cause-and-effect relationships, predict what will happen if you remove a bulb. Remove a light bulb. Record your observations.

Circuit	Diagram of Circuit	Observations
Series Circuit	bulb / bulb / battery	
Parallel Circuit		

Explain Your Results

1. Describe one difference between a series and parallel circuit.
2. Describe how you made your **predictions.** Compare your predictions and **observations.**

Go Further

Design and build other series and parallel circuits using components such as wires, batteries, and light bulbs. Diagram, test, and evaluate each circuit. Describe your circuits and tell what you learned to other students.

Focus on the BIG Idea   Electrical charges attract or repel each other. Electricity can be transformed to other forms of energy.

Lesson 1

How do charged objects behave?
- Objects with like charges push apart, or repel. Objects with unlike or neutral charges pull together, or attract.
- The pushing or pulling force is strongest close to the charged object.
- Static electricity is a buildup of electrical charges.

Lesson 2

How do electric charges move?
- An electric current is charges flowing through a closed path.
- A circuit has a power source, conductors, and resistors.
- A series circuit has only one path for the flowing charges.
- Electrical energy flowing through the circuit can be converted into heat and light.

Lesson 3

What are parallel circuits?
- A parallel circuit has at least two branches for the current.
- Products that need different amounts of current can be used at the same time on parallel circuits.
- Electrical energy flowing through a circuit can be converted into heat and light and also into the energy of motion.
- Some safety devices help protect people from electric shock, and other devices stop the flow of too much current.

Cross-Curricular Links

English–Language Arts

Building Vocabulary

Look back at pages 4–5 at the picture beside the term **series circuit**. Write a paragraph explaining how the picture shows that electrical energy is being converted to another form of energy.

Mathematics

Positive and Negative Numbers

Use one number cube to represent an object's positive charge and a different color number cube to represent its negative charge. Roll both cubes and compare the numbers. Is the object positively charged, negatively charge, or neutral? Explain how you know.

Challenge!

English–Language Arts

Integrated Circuits

Do research to find out more about circuits that are used in computers and other electronic devices. These circuits are called integrated circuits or computer chips. Give an oral report to your class to explain how these circuits are similar to and different from the circuits in this chapter.

English–Language Arts

Measuring Current and Resistance

How can the amount of current in a circuit be measured? How can resistance be measured? Use resource materials to find out. Then write an information report describing how current and resistance are measured.

Chapter 1 Review/Test

Use Vocabulary

electric charge (p. 9)	**resistance** (p. 15)
electric current (p. 14)	**series circuit** (p. 16)
parallel circuit (p. 20)	**static electricity** (p. 9)

Fill in the blanks with the correct vocabulary terms. If you have trouble answering a question, read the listed page again.

1. A(n) _____ has several paths through which electric charges can flow.

2. _____ is a property that limits the flow of current through a conductor.

3. Electric charges building up in an area or on an object is _____.

4. In a(n) _____, electric charges can move in only one loop.

5. A(n) _____ is a property of some parts of matter that is positive or negative.

6. _____ is electric charges in motion.

Think About It

7. Explain why the wires in electric circuits are often made of copper.

8. Why do most homes have parallel circuits rather than series circuits?

9. How does energy change when it passes through a light bulb filament?

10. **Process Skills** **Infer** You hold two balloons near each other. You feel a force pushing the balloons apart. What can you infer about the balloons?

11. **Form Hypotheses** You plan to investigate how rubbing a balloon with a piece of plastic wrap will affect its electrical charge. Write a testable hypothesis that describes what you expect would happen.

12. **Cause and Effect** Complete the graphic organizer to show what happens when a balloon becomes charged.

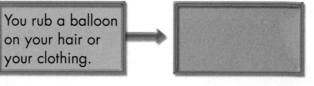

Cause	Effect
You rub a balloon on your hair or your clothing.	

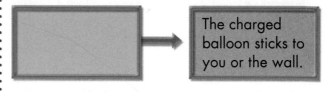

	The charged balloon sticks to you or the wall.

13. **Writing in Science**

Expository Write a newspaper article that explains how to build a simple parallel circuit that includes light bulbs. Explain the purpose of each part of the circuit and include a drawing or diagram with labels.

California Standards Practice

Write the letter of the correct answer.

14. Five light bulbs are wired on one circuit. Three bulbs are lit, two are not. What type of circuit is this?

A series

B parallel

C open

D short

Use the chart for Questions 15 and 16.

Material	Resistance
Glass	High
Hard rubber	High
Lead	Medium low
Silicon	Medium
Silver	Very low
Tungsten	Low

15. Which is the best material for insulating wires in a circuit?

A hard rubber

B lead

C silver

D tungsten

16. Which is the best conductor?

A glass

B lead

C silicon

D silver

17. When is the force between two charges strongest?

A when they are close together

B when they are far apart

C when electrons move farther apart

D when the charges flow

18. Why is electricity useful?

A Static electricity can make a spark.

B Insulators keep current in its path.

C Electric energy can change form.

D It makes balloons to stick to a wall.

19. A good energy source for a simple electric circuit is

A a light bulb.

B a copper wire.

C an extension cord.

D a battery.

20.

What is likely to happen soon?

A Thunder stops all moving charges.

B Lightning releases built-up charges.

C Lightning builds up charges.

D All charges gather in one cloud.

Everyday Uses of NASA Technology

Have you ever wondered where some of the devices that use electricity were developed? Many everyday objects started out as materials or technologies developed for the space program. Here are some examples:

Some people use satellite dishes to receive TV signals coming from satellites.

NASA developed a special bar-code system to keep track of parts used on spacecraft. We use bar codes to keep track of such things as library books and product sales.

The first smoke detectors were used in the Skylab space station in 1973 to detect poisons in the air. We use smoke detectors to warn us of fire. Some smoke detectors use batteries. Some are wired into the building's circuits.

Apollo astronauts first used cordless tools to collect samples from the Moon. This same technology has led to cordless vacuum cleaners, power drills, shrub trimmers, and grass shears.

Through technology, NASA developed a special joystick controller for the Apollo Lunar Rover. We use joystick controllers for certain electric household appliances, computer games, and vehicles for people with disabilities. Joysticks can be used to control electrical devices that are plugged in as well as those that run on stored power.

Lab zone Take-Home Activity

Sometimes people find new uses for ordinary objects. Take another look at electrical objects in your home. Develop a new use for one of these objects. Make a poster to share your idea with your class.

What is magnetism, and how is it useful?

electromagnet

Chapter 2 Vocabulary

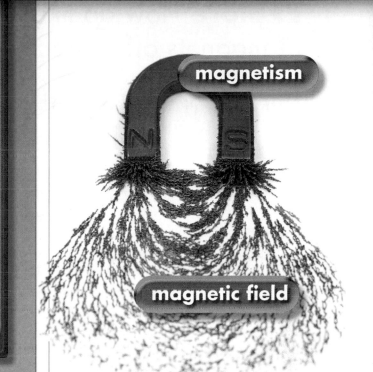

magnetism

magnetic field

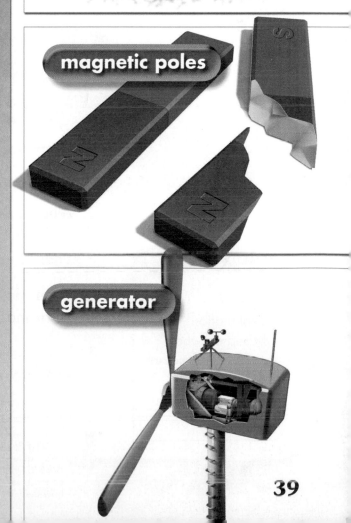

magnetic poles

generator

Explore How do like and unlike poles of magnets affect each other?

Use a pencil that has not been sharpened!

Materials

3 donut magnets

unsharpened pencil

What to Do

1 Put a magnet on the pencil.

2 Put another magnet on the pencil. **Observe.**

3 Flip the top magnet over. Observe.

4 Put a third magnet on the pencil. Observe.

Explain Your Results

1. What did you **observe** when unlike poles of 2 donut magnets were put together? when 2 like poles were put together

2. **Infer** How would the poles of 2 bar magnets affect each other?

3. Describe how your **inference** is different from your **observation.**

Process Skills

Scientific explanations are based on what scientists **observe** and how they interpret their observations.

DIGITAL Lab zone

4PS1.f Students know that magnets have two poles (north and south) and that like poles repel each other while unlike poles attract each other. **4IE6.a** Differentiate observation from inference (interpretation) and know scientists' explanations come partly from what they observe and partly from how they interpret their observations. (Also **4IE6.f**)

How to Read Science

Reading Skills

Main Idea and Details

The **main idea** is the most important idea discussed in a reading selection. It is the most important idea shown in a picture or model. As you read a selection or look at a picture, take note of **details** that make the main idea clearer. Some details may explain the main idea. Other details may give examples to support the main idea.

- The main idea of a paragraph is usually found in the topic sentence. It is often the first sentence of the paragraph.

- You can use what you **observe** and details that are familiar to you to make **inferences.**

Now read the following newspaper article.

Newspaper Article

Since it was first used on people in 1977, magnetic resonance imaging (MRI) has become a major problem-solving tool for doctors. MRIs use electromagnetic waves to make 3-D images of the body. Doctors can find problems inside the body without cutting into it. They are able to observe through bones and tissue. They are able to diagnose injuries and diseases.

Apply It!
Copy and complete the graphic organizer to show the **main idea** and **details** in the newspaper article. Use the graphic organizer to help you **infer** another reason MRIs are helpful.

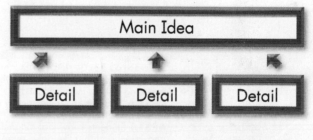

You Are There!

Excited, you hold your breath as the train starts to move. A whispery whoosh is all you hear. Within two minutes you are speeding toward the next stop at 300 kilometers per hour. Zoom! The train goes faster and faster as the landscape streaks by. Soon you are traveling almost 430 kph. It's as if you were flying—and, in a way, you are. A maglev train uses magnetic forces to zip along above the track without touching the track at all.

DIGITAL

What are magnetic fields?

Magnetism is a pulling or pushing force caused by the motion of electric charges. Magnets attract iron and have two poles, a north pole and a south pole. Like poles repel each other, and unlike poles attract each other.

Magnetism

Does the door of your refrigerator look like a combination scrapbook and message center? Papers, photos, notes, and reminders may be held in place by many colorful refrigerator magnets. Magnets are objects that attract iron, steel, and some other metals. This attraction is what makes the magnets cling to your refrigerator.

All magnets have the property of magnetism. **Magnetism** is a force that acts on moving electric charges and on magnetic materials that are near a magnet. Some minerals, such as lodestone, are magnetic. Magnets can also be made using electricity. You will learn more about this in Lesson 3.

Holding papers to a refrigerator is no big job, but what about a heavy maglev train? How do magnets support the train so that it seems to float on air? Electric current that is flowing through the train tracks produces enough magnetic force to lift the entire train! The pushing and pulling force between magnets also moves the train along the track.

1. ✓**Checkpoint** What is magnetism?

2. Name two materials that are attracted by a magnet.

Magnetic forces lift and propel this maglev train as it speeds along about one centimeter above the track.

Magnetic Field

You may have seen a paper clip move across a desk toward a powerful magnet. How can the magnet affect an object that it doesn't touch? Each magnet has a magnetic field around it. A **magnetic field** is the space around a magnet in which magnetic forces operate. The magnetic field extends out in all directions from a magnet. The exact shape of the field depends on the shape of the magnet.

Magnetic fields are invisible, but you can detect their shapes by using iron filings. Look at the patterns of iron filings near the large U-shaped magnet. The filings line up in the magnetic field. Notice how the lines of filings curve outward from the ends of the magnet. This shows the location and shape of the magnetic field.

Iron filings near a U-shaped magnet show that the magnetic field is strongest near the poles.

Iron filings show the magnetic field around each magnet.

Magnetic Poles

You can see many filings gathered at the ends of the magnet. The two ends of a magnet are called its **magnetic poles.** The north magnetic pole is pulled to the north by Earth's magnetic field. The south magnetic pole is pulled to the south by Earth's magnetic field. The magnetic field is strongest at the magnet's poles. The field gets weaker as you move away from the poles, so the filings are farther apart.

Fields, Forces, and Filings

Look at the pictures at the right. The iron filings show the shape of each magnet's magnetic field. Compare the magnetic fields of the bar and horseshoe magnets. For each magnet, you find the most filings where the magnetic field is strongest. The pattern around each magnet is slightly different. But each pattern spreads out from one pole and curves around the magnet to the other pole.

Iron filings near a bar magnet show the magnetic field is strongest near the poles.

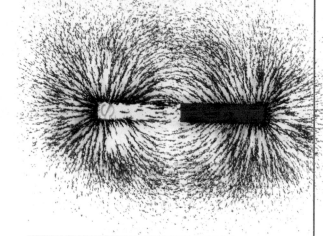

DIGITAL Look for Active Art animations at www.pearsonsuccessnet.com

A horseshoe magnet has a magnetic field that looks most like that of the large U-shaped magnet.

1. ✔ **Checkpoint** What are magnetic poles?

2. **Main Idea and Details** What is a magnetic field? Explain the main idea and give at least three supporting details.

How Magnetic Poles Behave

You read in Chapter 1 that unlike electric charges attract each other and like charges repel each other. A magnet's poles also behave in this way. Like poles repel each other, and unlike poles attract each other.

To observe this, you need two magnets. If you place a north pole next to another north pole, they are pushed apart by the force of their magnetic fields. But if you put a north pole near a south pole, the opposite poles are pulled toward each other. The pictures on the next page show magnets placed next to each other. Iron filings show their magnetic fields. Look at the magnetic fields that form when like and unlike poles are placed together.

You can also feel this property if you use two magnetic sheets, such as those used in flat, refrigerator magnets. Each sheet has north and south poles arranged in a special way. If you slide one sheet over another, you can feel them repel and attract. The like poles repel each other, and the unlike poles attract each other.

Thin, cardlike refrigerator magnets have rows of small magnets in very narrow strips.

A U-shaped magnet has two poles. If it is broken, the pieces are no longer U-shaped. But each piece still has a north and a south pole.

Each piece of a broken bar magnet has two opposite poles.

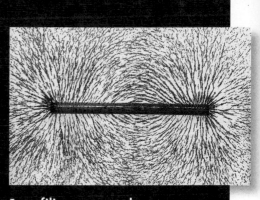

Iron filings near a bar magnet show the magnetic field is strongest near the poles.

The north pole of one bar magnet attracts the south pole of another bar magnet. The iron filings show the magnetic field.

Broken Magnets

What do you think will happen if you break a magnet into two pieces? Yes, you will get two magnets, but the rest of the answer might be a surprise. You won't get a single magnetic pole. Instead, each new magnet will have a north pole and a south pole. In fact, you can never have one kind of pole without the other! North and south magnetic poles are like the two sides of a coin.

✓ Lesson Review

1. How do the poles of a magnet behave when placed near the poles of another magnet?

2. If you break a bar magnet in two pieces, will the ends formed by the break attract or repel each other? Explain.

3. ✎ **Writing in Science Summarize**
   Write a paragraph summarizing how horseshoe and bar magnets have different-shaped magnetic fields.

Two north poles repel each other. The iron filings show the magnetic field.

Lesson 2

What are magnetic effects?

Earth acts as a giant magnet with north and south magnetic poles and a huge magnetic field. A compass can be made from a floating or suspended magnet that is free to align with Earth's magnetic poles.

Compasses and the World's Largest Magnet

Have you ever used a compass? Its needle always moves so that one end points north and the other points south. Many ancient sailors used compasses successfully without knowing why they worked. Christopher Columbus used a compass when he crossed the Atlantic Ocean. About 400 years ago, English scientist William Gilbert suggested that the world's largest magnet is Earth itself! He proposed that Earth is a huge magnet, surrounded by an enormous magnetic field.

Why does Earth act like a magnet? Scientists are not sure of the answer. After all, no one has actually seen the inside of our planet. However, scientists use what they have observed to infer that Earth's outer core is made of iron so hot that it has melted. They think that as Earth rotates, electric currents flow in this liquid iron. The flowing current creates a magnetic field. Earth's inner core is probably solid iron that is also very hot. It doesn't melt because of extremely high pressure.

Magnetic Minerals

Some rocks and minerals are natural magnets. Since ancient times, people have noticed the magnetic properties of these rocks. The word *magnet* comes from a Greek phrase meaning "Magnesian rock." Magnesia, a part of ancient Greece, was famous long ago for having large amounts of magnetite, Earth's most magnetic mineral. Magnetite is also called lodestone. Because pieces of magnetite will point north and south, ancient sailors used lodestones as compasses. Today, Magnesia is part of Turkey.

The magnetic field of this stone attracts metal pins.

Standards Focus 4PS1.b Students know how to build a simple compass and use it to detect magnetic effects, including Earth's magnetic field.
4IE6.a Differentiate observation from inference (interpretation) and know scientists' explanations come partly from what they observe and partly from how they interpret their observations.
4IE6.f Follow a set of written instructions for a scientific investigation.

Earth's Magnetic Poles

Like those of all magnets, Earth's magnetic field is strongest at its poles. Its magnetic poles are not at the same place as its geographic poles. The geographic poles are on the axis, the invisible line around which Earth rotates. The magnetic pole in the Northern Hemisphere is in Canada, about 1,000 kilometers (600 miles) from the geographic North Pole. In the Southern Hemisphere, the magnetic pole is in the ocean near Antarctica.

Earth is like a giant magnet surrounded by a huge magnetic field.

1. ✓**Checkpoint** Why is it correct to say that Earth is a giant magnet?

2. ✎ **Writing in Science Narrative** In the Northern Hemisphere, particles moving in Earth's magnetic field cause auroras called the Northern Lights. Find out more about auroras. Write a paragraph describing an aurora and why you would remember seeing it.

Compasses

You are hiking in the woods. You know that your campsite is somewhere to the east. But you are not sure which way is east. A compass can help you find your way. A compass needle is a tiny, lightweight magnet. It is mounted so that it can turn freely inside the compass. Wherever you are on Earth, one end of a compass needle will point toward Earth's magnetic north pole.

Why does a compass needle always point toward the north and south magnetic poles? The needle is attracted by Earth's magnetic field. Think of the picture with the lines showing Earth's magnetic field. The lines run north and south between the poles. A compass needle lines up with the magnetic field.

Now suppose that you are walking in the forest with your trusty compass. You are traveling east, toward your campsite, taking great care to keep the N on the compass under the end of the needle that points north. Suddenly, you see the needle swing around and point west. How could this be? You remember that some rocks are magnetic. You keep walking, and soon the needle swings back toward north. Whew!

A Magnetic Rock

But now you are curious about magnetic rocks. So you backtrack, testing the compass against each rock along the trail. Sure enough, you find a large rock that pulls the compass needle away from north. You have detected the magnetic effect of magnetite! Why did the needle swing? The magnetic field of a nearby magnet, the magnetite in the rock, was stronger than Earth's magnetic field. The stronger field attracted the compass needle.

A compass needle normally points north and south because of Earth's magnetic field.

A bar magnet brought near the compass changes the direction in which the compass needle points.

Earth's Magnetic Field

Earth's magnetic field can be detected by any magnet, not just a compass. Just suspend the magnet so that it swings freely. You can hang the magnet by tying a string or rubber band around it. In a short time, the magnet will line up with Earth's magnetic lines of force. The ends of a bar magnet or faces of a donut magnet will point north and south.

But how can you be sure which pole points north and which points south? Compare your hanging magnet with a compass. Make sure that the compass is far enough away from the magnet so as not to pull the compass needle away from north. The north end or face of the magnet points the same way as the north end of the compass. You can then label that end of the magnet *N*. Now your magnet can be a compass!

If you suspend a magnet so that it can turn freely, its poles will line up with Earth's magnetic field. Remember, if the magnet is too close to a compass, the magnet's field will cause the compass needle to move.

The axis of the hole in a ring magnet aligns with Earth's north and south magnetic poles.

This side is the south pole. The north pole is the other side of the magnet.

1. **✔Checkpoint** Why do the ends of a compass needle point north and south?

2. How can you find the poles on a donut or ring magnet?

How to Make a Compass

Ancient people floated a lodestone on a stick in water to make a compass. But you don't have to find a magnetic rock to make a simple compass. A floating needle can act as a compass.

This simple compass was made with a needle, a magnet, a bowl of water, and a piece of sponge or cork. First, the needle was rubbed on the magnet. It was moved quickly and always in the same direction. The needle gained a magnetic field.

Rubbing a needle on a magnet can make the needle into a temporary magnet.

Then, the needle was placed on the piece of sponge or cork. The sponge or cork floated in the water, allowing the needle to turn freely. Or, a very small bar magnet could have been placed directly on the floating piece. The water had to be still, and the needle had to be parallel to the water's surface.

A magnetized needle will line up with Earth's magnetic field. It will point north and south. A commercial compass will show the direction of magnetic north—the north end of the needle in the floating compass.

A freely floating magnetized needle will point toward Earth's magnetic north pole.

A small bar magnet can be placed on the cork instead of a needle.

Finding Your Way

How does a floating compass show directions? Labels *north*, *south*, *east*, and *west* are on the edges of the bowl. Then the bowl is turned so that the north end of the needle or magnet points to the "north" mark on the bowl. It is hard to use this compass on a hike, but it works just like a smaller commercial compass!

Lesson Review

1. Why must the compass needle be able to move easily?

2. How can a compass be used to detect magnetic effects?

3. **Writing in Science** **Expository** Suppose that you are going to teach a group of third graders how to make a compass. Write a set of directions for them. Make sure your explanation is clear and easy to follow.

How are electric currents and magnetic fields related?

Electric current produces magnetic fields through the motion of electric charges. Likewise, magnetic fields produce electric current. An electromagnet is made by passing electric current through a coiled wire.

Electric Current Produces a Magnetic Field

In 1820, a Danish scientist named Hans Christian Oersted was running electric current through a wire. He noticed that the magnetic needle on a nearby compass moved each time he turned on the current. He wondered why that happened. Oersted realized that the flowing electric charges caused a magnetic field. Clearly, electricity and magnetism have a lot in common.

The two pictures below show how an electric current affects compasses. When the current flows, the compass needles line up with the lines of a magnetic field.

No current is flowing. All compass needles point north.

Here the compass needles line up with the magnetic field caused by the flowing current.

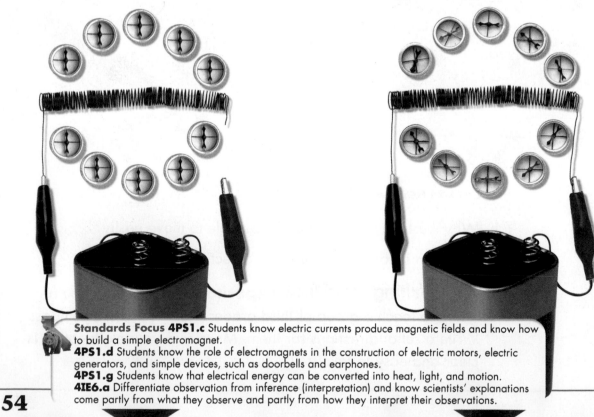

Standards Focus 4PS1.c Students know electric currents produce magnetic fields and know how to build a simple electromagnet.
4PS1.d Students know the role of electromagnets in the construction of electric motors, electric generators, and simple devices, such as doorbells and earphones.
4PS1.g Students know that electrical energy can be converted into heat, light, and motion.
4IE6.a Differentiate observation from inference (interpretation) and know scientists' explanations come partly from what they observe and partly from how they interpret their observations.

Moving Magnets Produce Electricity

After Oersted's work, scientists learned more that helped them explain how electricity and magnetism are related. In 1831, British scientist Michael Faraday discovered that moving a magnet inside a wire coil produces an electric current. He invented a device called a dynamo. It uses a moving magnet to produce electricity.

You can see how a magnet produces electricity. The meter shown here measures the amount of electric current. A magnet inside the coil of wire doesn't seem to do much. The meter reading is zero. No current is flowing.

But what happens if the magnet is moved back and forth? Then, the needle on the meter swings left and right, away from zero. The movement of the magnet and its magnetic field causes electric current to flow in the coil and through the meter.

What causes the electric current? Recall that magnetism is caused by the motion of electric charges. Electric charges in motion are also the cause of electric current. You can conclude that magnetism and electricity are closely related.

The magnet is not moving. The meter shows that no current is flowing.

Moving the magnet back and forth inside the coil produces an electric current.

1. **✓ Checkpoint** How are electric current and magnetic fields related?

2. What happens to the electric current when you stop moving the magnet inside the coil?

This electromagnet picks up several paper clips.

Electromagnets

Each coil of wire in the pictures that you just saw is the simplest kind of electromagnet. An **electromagnet** is a coil of wire with many loops through which an electric current passes. The moving current creates a magnetic field.

You can change the strength of an electromagnet in several ways. You can make the magnetic field stronger by putting an iron or steel bar inside the coil of wire. The thicker the bar, the stronger the electromagnet will be. You can also add more coils of wire. You can wrap the coils more tightly.

This battery produces a small amount of electric current and a weak magnetic field.

Current flowing through the coil changes some energy to heat. The heat makes the mat change color.

To make an electromagnet stronger you can also use a stronger current. This could mean connecting more batteries or using a more powerful battery. The pictures show what happens when the amount of current changes.

This stronger battery can produce a larger amount of current.

The stronger current boosts the magnetic force. The color of the mat shows that some of the energy in this circuit has also been converted to heat. Compare the two electromagnets. Which do you think would pick up more paper clips?

1. ✔**Checkpoint** Describe how to build an electromagnet.

2. **Main Idea and Details** List three ways to increase the strength of an electromagnet.

Applications of Electromagnets

Did you use a computer recently? If you did, you used an electromagnet. Of course, if you were to look inside a computer, you wouldn't find an iron bar with wire wrapped around it. But the computer's hard drive uses electromagnets.

The bar with a coil of wire is a simple electromagnet. Electromagnets are different sizes and shapes. They may be made from high-tech materials. But all of them produce a magnetic field only when an electric current passes through them.

Flashlight Without Batteries
This flashlight uses an electromagnet for power. When you shake the tube, a magnet moves through a coil of wire. This causes an electric current that powers the light.

Magnetic Resonance Imaging (MRI)
An MRI machine lets doctors observe organs and tissues inside the body. The machine produces magnetic fields that affect some particles in the body. A computer uses these particles to make images. An MRI machine is safer than many other ways to observe organs and tissues inside the body. However, its magnetic field is very strong. Metal objects may be attracted to the magnet! People usually leave keys, jewelry, and other metal objects in another room.

Computer Hard Drive
A hard drive is coated with a magnetic material. When you save a file, the magnetic fields change quickly. The patterns they make "write" the information on the hard drive. Magnetic patterns also let you get the information you saved.

Scrap Metal Lifter
This giant electromagnet lifts a pile of scrap iron and steel. The iron and steel may weigh many times what the lifter weighs. The huge face of the lifter is one pole of a gigantic bar magnet. This magnet is so strong that it needs special parts to stop the magnetic field after the current has been turned off.

✓ Lesson Review

1. Name three different kinds of electromagnets.

2. What causes current to flow in the flashlight without batteries?

3. ✏ **Writing in Science**

   Descriptive Write an advertisement for an invention that uses an electromagnet. Describe how your invention uses an electromagnet. Explain why your invention is useful.

59

Lesson 4

How are electromagnets used?

Electromagnets can convert electrical energy to other forms of energy. Electromagnets can also work with magnets and wire coils to produce motion in motors and generators.

Electromagnets in Sound Devices

Your neighbor turns up the volume to listen to his latest CD. The sound coming from the large speakers rattles the floor and walls. How do the speakers make so much noise?

You may not realize that electromagnets are part of many common electronic gadgets and sound devices. Electromagnets in the speakers produce a magnetic field. As the amount of current changes, so does the magnetic field. The changes cause motion, or vibrations in the speakers. The vibrations make the sound waves you hear.

How a Doorbell Works

Button—Pressing the button closes the electric circuit. Current flows to the...

Transformer—This device controls the amount of current that is sent to the...

Electromagnet—Electricity flowing in the coil of wire magnetizes the electromagnet. This pulls up the...

Contact Arm—The arm is attached to a metal clapper that hits the...

Bell—This makes the sound.

Standards Focus 4PS1.0 Electricity and magnetism are related effects that have many useful applications in everyday life. As a basis for understanding this concept:
4PS1.d Students know the role of electromagnets in the construction of electric motors, electric generators, and simple devices, such as doorbells and earphones.
4PS1.g Students know that electrical energy can be converted to heat, light, and motion.

Earphones

In a set of earphones, a metal disc is located in front of an electromagnet in each earphone. Changes in the electric current make the magnetism weaker or stronger. The changes in the strength of the magnetism make the disc vibrate. The vibrations produce the sound waves that you hear.

How a Speaker Works

As electromagnets turn on and off rapidly, the magnet pushes and pulls on the speaker cone. This causes the cone to vibrate. These vibrations produce sound waves.

Earphones turn electric current into sound waves.

magnet

speaker cone

1. **✔Checkpoint** How do electromagnets change electric energy into motion and sound in a speaker?

2. Explain how energy changes form and makes a doorbell ring.

Electric Energy Changing to Motion

Think of things that spin when you close a circuit by flipping a switch. You might think of a fan or a blender. These electrical objects have motors. A motor changes electrical energy into mechanical energy. *Mechanical energy* is the energy involved in motion. Computers, CD and DVD players, and some toy cars have motors with many parts.

Simple Electric Motor

A simple motor, however, can have only a few parts. Look at the photo at the right. You see a battery, a magnet, a coil with seven loops, and some wire. You also see parts that connect or hold the other parts together. You are looking at a simple motor. The coil of wire in the center is called a *rotor*. It spins. But what makes the rotor spin? The electric current from the battery passes through the rotor. The current creates a magnetic field in the rotor. Like any magnet, the rotor's magnetic field has two poles. The poles of the permanent magnet attract and repel the poles of the rotor's magnetic field. This makes the rotor turn.

Inside this fan, an electric motor turns a rod called an axle. The axle is attached to the wheel of fan blades. The fan blades spin at the same rate as the motor.

The insulation has been removed from only one side of the axle.

Going Around in Circles

But after the rotor turns halfway, why doesn't it change directions? Look carefully at the axles—the wires connected to each side of the rotor. The insulation has been completely removed from one of the wires. Only one side of the insulation has been removed from the other wire. The insulation acts as a switch and briefly stops the flow of charges in the spinning coil. But before the coil stops spinning, the bare wire closes the circuit allowing charges to flow again.

So how does the motion of the motor get changed into the spinning motion of a fan or blender? Find the axle in the photo of the motor. When the rotor spins, it turns the axle. In some objects, especially those with more powerful motors, the axle is attached to something that spins. The axle turns whatever is connected to it, such as the blades of a fan or a blender.

Battery

Paper clips are the wires that connect the battery to the axle. This allows current to flow.

Permanent Magnet

On this part of the axle, insulation has been completely removed.

Rotor

1. ✔**Checkpoint** How does an electric motor convert electrical energy to motion?

2. 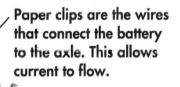 **Writing in Science** **Descriptive** In your own words, describe in detail how to build the motor shown above. Combine information from the picture and the words.

Math in Science

An Electromagnet's Strength

There are different ways to change the strength of an electromagnet. One way is to add or remove coils. Another way is to change the amount of current. You can make the electromagnet stronger by putting an iron core inside the coil. A larger core will make the electromagnet even stronger.

A bar graph can help you compare the strength of electromagnets. The purple bar shows the number of paper clips that an electromagnet picked up. The other bars show the number of paper clips that it picked up after it was changed in just one way. You can see that the green bar for changing the current is twice as long as the purple bar for the original magnet. This shows that the amount of current was doubled, perhaps by increasing the number of batteries.

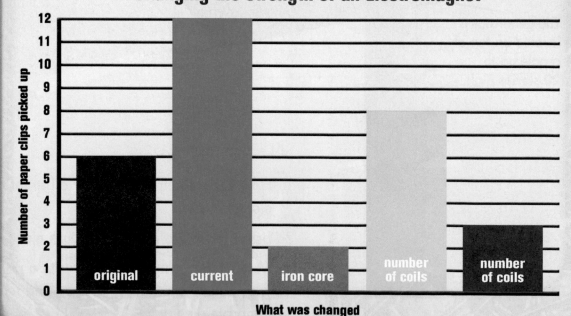

Changing the Strength of an Electromagnet

Number of paper clips picked up (y-axis: 0–12)

original, current, iron core, number of coils, number of coils

What was changed

DIGITAL

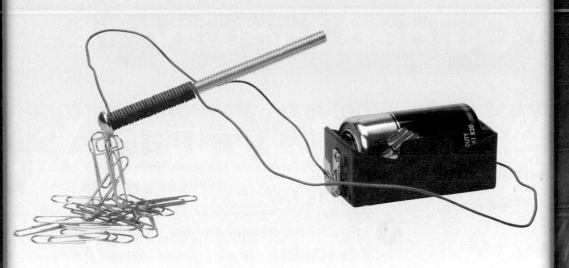

Use the data displayed in the bar graph to answer the questions. For each question, explain how you can find the answer by comparing the lengths of bars.

1. The number of coils was changed in two different ways. How does the number of coils for each change compare to the number in the original electromagnet?

2. Did the original electromagnet have an iron core?

Lab zone **Take-Home Activity**

You can change a nonmagnetic screwdriver into a magnet. Do this activity with an adult. Use a 6-volt battery or a battery holder with four "D" cells, and about 5m of insulated copper wire. Wrap the wire in tight coils around a pencil, leaving about 30 cm at each end. Attach one wire end to a battery terminal. Replace the pencil with a screwdriver. Touch the loose wire end to the other terminal for just 10 seconds—not more! Record how many paper clips your screwdriver picks up.

Investigate What is an electromagnet?

Wear safety goggles.
Disconnect wires from
battery if any parts feel warm.

Be careful!

Materials

safety goggles

spool of wire
(whole class use)

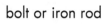

metric ruler

bolt or iron rod

battery in
battery holder

20 small paper clips

wire cutter and stripper
(whole class use)

Process Skills

Careful **estimates**
and accurate
measurements
can help you
obtain reliable
results.

What to Do

1 Start 40 centimeters from one end of the
wire. Coil the wire 30 times around the
bolt near its head.

You need a 2 meter length of insulated wire. First **estimate**
how much you need. Then **measure** and cut the wire. Follow
your teacher's directions for additional preparation.

Leave a 40 centimeter piece uncoiled.

30 coils

2 Hold the bolt's head near a paper clip.
Record your **observations.**

30 coils
(no battery)

4PS1.c Students know electric currents produce magnetic fields and know how
to build a simple electromagnet. **4IE6.b** Measure and estimate the weight,
length, or volume of objects. **4IE6.c** Formulate and justify predictions based on
cause-and-effect relationships. **4IE6.d** Conduct multiple trials to test a prediction
and draw conclusions about the relationships between predictions and results.
4IE6.e Construct and interpret graphs from measurements. (Also **4IE6.f**)

3 Attach both ends of the wire to the battery holder. **Measure** the strength of your electromagnet by finding how many paper clips it can pick up. Remove a wire from the battery holder. Repeat twice.

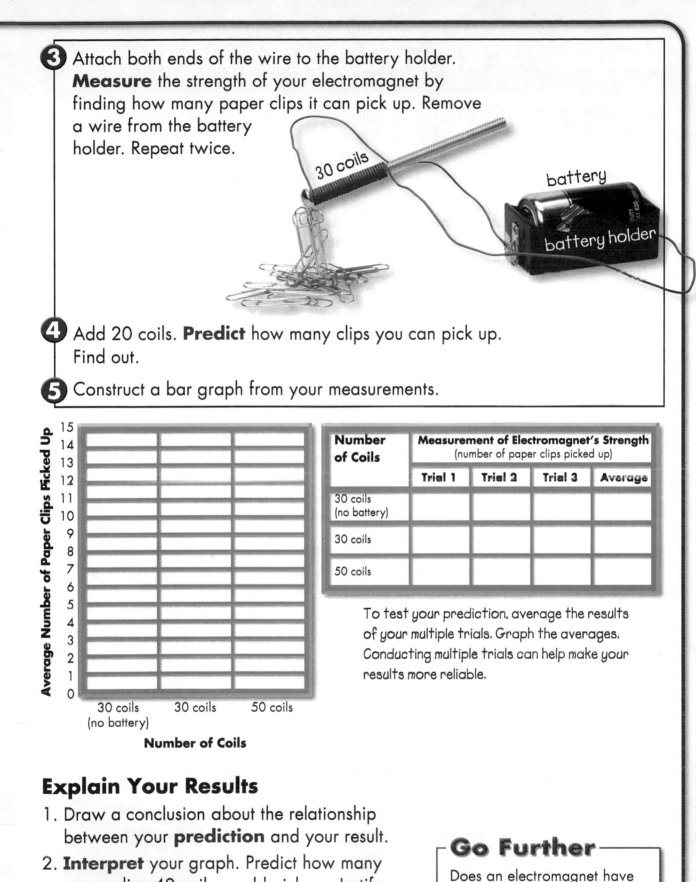

30 coils

battery

battery holder

4 Add 20 coils. **Predict** how many clips you can pick up. Find out.

5 Construct a bar graph from your measurements.

Number of Coils	Measurement of Electromagnet's Strength (number of paper clips picked up)			
	Trial 1	**Trial 2**	**Trial 3**	**Average**
30 coils (no battery)				
30 coils				
50 coils				

To test your prediction, average the results of your multiple trials. Graph the averages. Conducting multiple trials can help make your results more reliable.

Explain Your Results

1. Draw a conclusion about the relationship between your **prediction** and your result.

2. **Interpret** your graph. Predict how many paper clips 40 coils would pick up. Justify your **prediction** based on cause-and-effect relationships.

Go Further

Does an electromagnet have 2 poles? Use a compass to find out.

Chapter 2 Review/Test

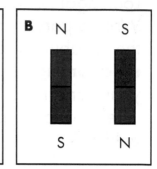

Use Vocabulary

electromagnet (p. 56)	**magnetic poles** (p. 44)
generator (p. 64)	**magnetism** (p. 43)
magnetic field (p. 44)	

Fill in the blanks with the correct vocabulary terms. If you have trouble answering a question, read the listed page again.

1. Because of Earth's _____, a compass needle points north-south.

2. _____ is a force that acts on moving electrical charges near a magnet.

3. One advantage of a(n) _____ is that its magnetic field can be turned off.

4. A(n) _____ converts mechanical energy into electric energy.

5. The _____ of a magnet are labeled north and south.

Think About It

6. How do magnetic poles show magnetic force?

7. How can a compass be used to detect Earth's magnetic field?

8. How are both motors and generators examples of energy changing form?

9. **Process Skills** **Predict** What would happen if the coils in a generator stopped spinning?

10. **Infer** Which pair of bar magnets will attract each other? Explain your answer.

A	N	N
	S	S

B	N	S
	S	N

11. **Main Idea and Details** Complete the graphic organizer by writing details or examples that support the main idea.

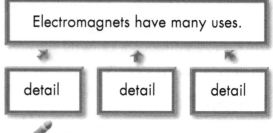

Electromagnets have many uses.

| detail | detail | detail |

12. **Writing in Science** **Descriptive** Write directions that describe how to build and test a simple electromagnet. Include a list of materials and instructions in numbered steps.

California Standards Practice

Write the letter of the correct answer.

13. Which change will make an electromagnet stronger?

A using a smaller core

B removing the metal core

C adding coils

D moving coils farther apart

14. A bar magnet is hanging from a string. What happens if you hold a compass near the magnet?

A The magnet spins in circles.

B The compass needle spins in circles.

C The compass needle does not move.

D The magnet attracts the compass needle.

15. Where do iron filings near a magnet cluster most strongly?

A around Earth's field lines

B around the south pole

C around the north pole

D around the magnet's poles

16. Electromagnets in earphones change electrical energy into

A thin paper disks.

B motion and sound.

C radio waves.

D magnetic poles.

17. Which is magnetic?

A turbine

B cork

C Magnesia

D lodestone

18. How can you magnetize a needle ?

A Rub it on a magnet.

B Wrap it with coils of wire.

C Float it on a sponge.

D Suspend it by a string.

19. Maglev trains use the power of

A wind.

B electromagnets.

C flowing water.

D compasses.

20. What do the compass needles in the drawing show?

A Current produces a magnetic field.

B Earth has a curved magnetic field.

C The coil needs an iron bolt.

D No current is flowing.

Experiment Can you change the poles of an electromagnet?

Electric currents produce magnetic fields. When electric current flows through an electromagnet, the electromagnet becomes a temporary magnet. It has many properties similar to those of a permanent magnet. For example, it has a north pole and a south pole. You can show this with a compass. However, when the electric current stops flowing, the electromagnet is no longer a magnet. What might happen if the direction the electric current flows is reversed?

Materials

safety goggles
and metric ruler

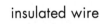

insulated wire

iron or steel bolt or rod

battery and
battery holder

directional compass

Process Skills

A **hypothesis** is a statement that answers a question and that can be tested by an **experiment.**

Ask a question.

Does the direction the electric current flows through an electromagnet affect the locations of the poles?

State a hypothesis.

If the direction the electrons move through an electromagnet is reversed, then do the locations of the poles change or remain the same? Write your **hypothesis.**

Identify and control variables.

You will change the direction the electrons move through an electromagnet. You will observe the locations of the poles on an electromagnet before and after you change the direction the electrons move. Keep everything else the same.

DIGITAL Lab zone

4PS1.c Students know electric currents produce magnetic fields and know how to build a simple electromagnet. **4IE6.b** Measure and estimate the weight, length, or volume of objects. **4IE6.d** Conduct multiple trials to test a prediction and draw conclusions about the relationships between predictions and results. (Also **4IE6.f**)

Test your hypothesis.

1 Make an electromagnet. Make sure you use 120 cm of wire. **Measure** the length. Then start about 20 cm from one end of the wire. Coil the long part around the bolt 30 times.

2 Make Circuit A. Connect one end of the wire to the positive (+) side of the battery holder. Then connect the other end of the wire to the negative (−) side.

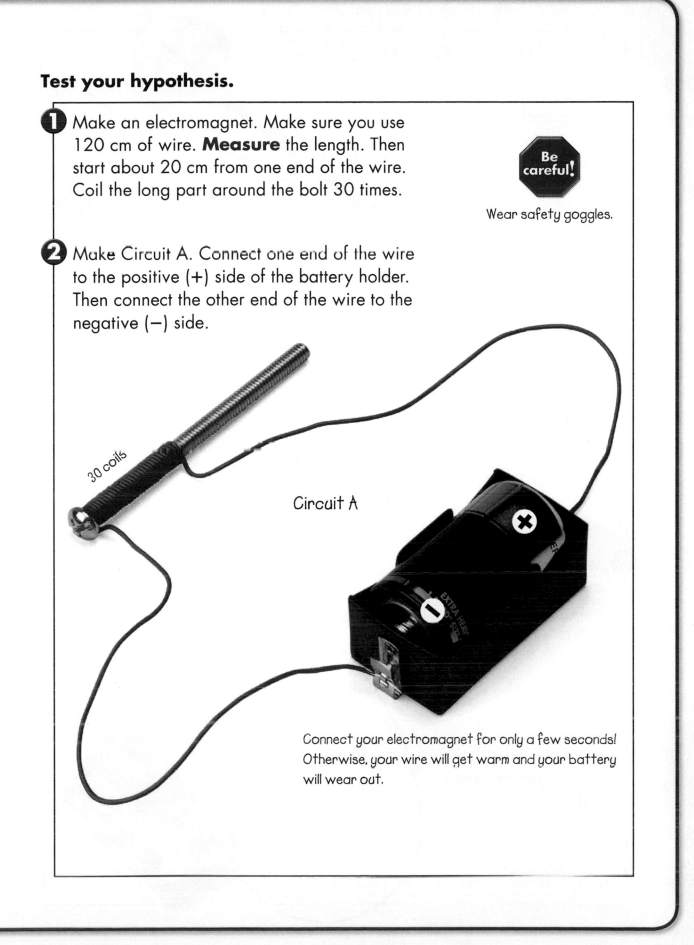

30 coils

Circuit A

Connect your electromagnet for only a few seconds! Otherwise, your wire will get warm and your battery will wear out.

3 Use a compass to find the poles of the electromagnet. The north-seeking end of the compass will point to the north pole of the electromagnet. Disconnect the ends of the wire.

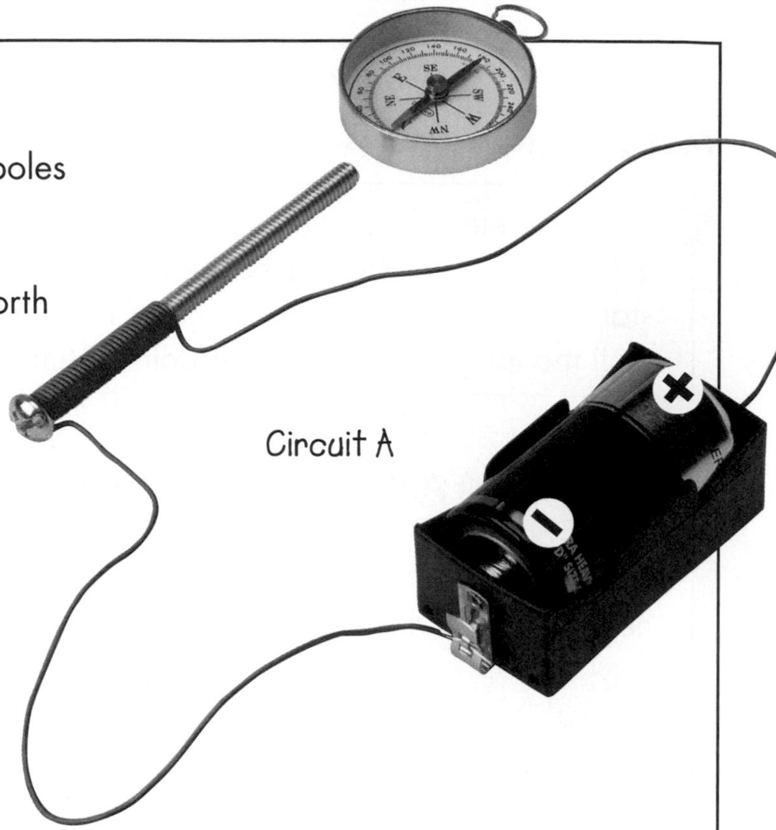

Circuit A

4 Electrons move through the wire from the negative (−) side of a battery to the positive (+) side. In the chart on the next page, finish the arrows to show the direction the electrons move in circuit A. Label the north and south poles on the electromagnet.

5 Repeat steps 2 to 4, but make Circuit B. Disconnect the electromagnet. Turn it around and reconnect it.

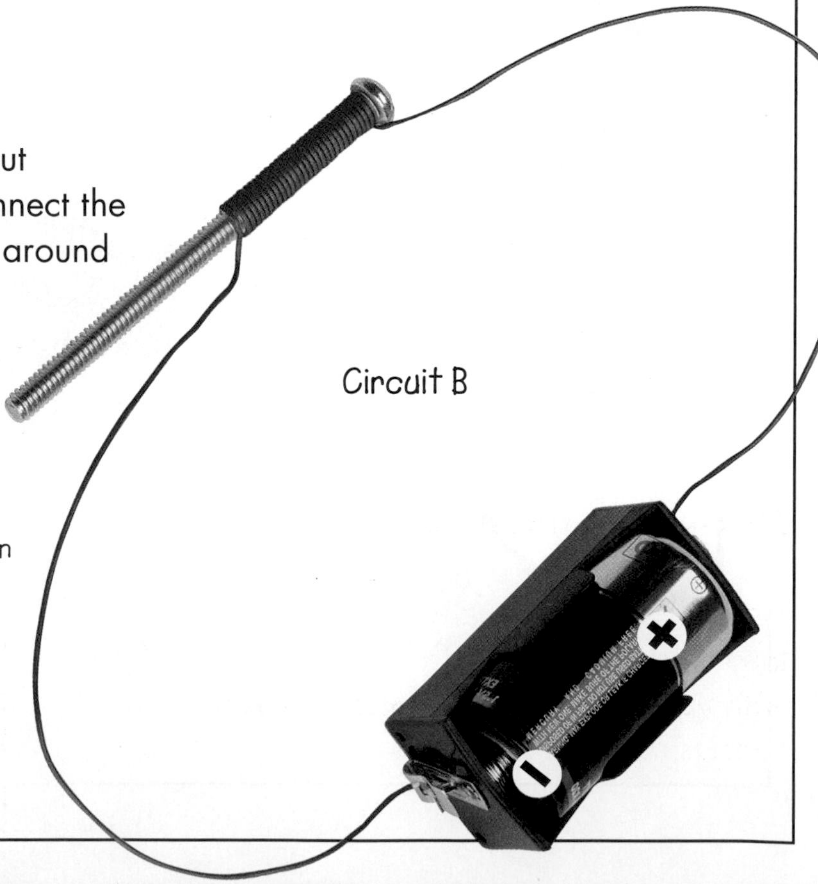

Circuit B

Repeat the steps twice. Conducting multiple trials can help make your results more reliable.

Collect and record your data.

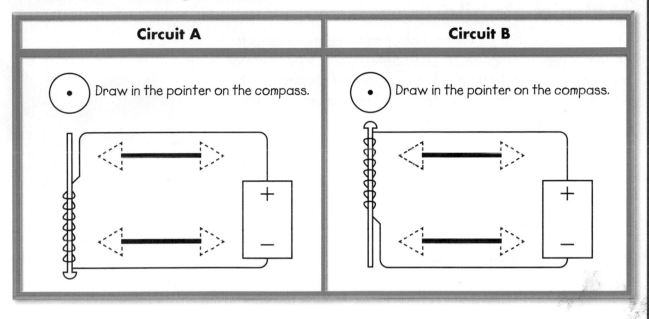

Circuit A	Circuit B
Draw in the pointer on the compass.	Draw in the pointer on the compass.

Complete the diagram to show the direction the electrons move through the electromagnet.
Label the poles of the electromagnet.

Interpret your data.
Analyze the drawings that show the data from your **experiment.** Compare the circuits.
What direction are the electrons moving in each circuit—from the bolt's head toward the bolt's tip or from the tip toward the head? Is the bolt's head a north or south pole in Circuit A? in Circuit B?

State your conclusion.
Explain how reversing the direction the electrons move through an electromagnet affects the locations of its poles. Compare your hypothesis with your results. **Communicate** your conclusion.

Go Further

How do the poles of 2 electromagnets affect each other? Make a plan to investigate this question or develop a question of your own. With your teacher's permission, conduct a careful investigation to answer the question.

Show What You Know

Make a Mobile

Make a mobile that shows how electrically charged objects attract or repel one another. Use lightweight pieces of paper, balloons, or other materials that can become charged and hung by a string. Keep a sample of what you used to charge the items hanging in your mobile.

Make a Prediction

Use wire and a power source to make a simple circuit. The current flowing through a wire makes a magnetic field. The field causes the needle of a compass to point a certain way. Predict what will happen to the compass needle if the current flows through the wire in the opposite direction. Use a compass to check your prediction. Make a poster that shows what happened.

Write a Poem

Write a poem about a magnet's poles. Include a magnet's north pole and a magnet's south pole. Tell which poles attract and which poles repel. Here are some tips to help you write your poem.

- A poem is written in lines.
- A poem has a nice sound when you read it.

Read More About Physical Sciences

Look for other books about Physical Sciences in your library-media center. One book you may want to read is:

Electricity
by Steve Parker

This book tells you about some of the early ideas and discoveries that helped explain the force of electricity. You'll also read how electricity is produced and how it is related to magnetism. You will see examples that show some of the ways electricity is used today.

Science Fair Projects

Full Inquiry

Using Scientific Methods

1. Ask a question.
2. State a hypothesis.
3. Identify and control variables.
4. Test your hypothesis.
5. Collect and record your data.
6. Interpret your data.
7. State your conclusion.
8. Go further.

Which battery lasts longest?

Batteries have different life spans.

Idea: You will need several brands of new batteries and a flashlight for each brand. Make sure that the flashlights all have the same type of bulb. They must also use the same type and the same number of batteries. Turn on all flashlights. Time how long each battery brand keeps the flashlight lit.

What shape does a magnetic field have?

Magnetic fields are three dimensional.

Idea: Use bar magnets to attract iron filings suspended in cooking oil inside a clear plastic jar. Bar magnets can be used to show the shapes of magnetic fields. Place one pole of a bar magnet at the side of the jar. Then try the other pole. Then try two bar magnets placed opposite each other. Make drawings and describe the patterns formed by the iron filings.

What materials conduct electricity?

Some materials are conductors and some are insulators.

Idea: Set up a series circuit by using a battery, wires, and a flashlight bulb. Disconnect one wire from the bulb. Connect one end of another wire in its place. Test different materials by touching the loose ends of the wires to two sides of an object. Observe which materials conduct enough electric current to light the bulb. Classify the tested materials.

Unit A California Standards Practice

Write the letter of the correct answer.

1. **A compass needle points toward which place on Earth?**

   A north geographic pole

   B north magnetic pole

   C south geographic pole

   D Magnesia

2. **The diagram below shows a simple circuit.**

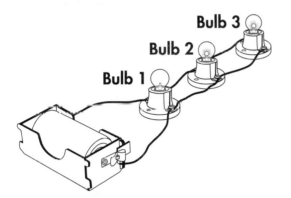

Bulb 3
Bulb 2
Bulb 1

   What will happen if light bulb 2 burns out?

   A Only light bulb 1 will light.

   B Only light bulb 3 will light.

   C Light bulbs 1 and 3 will light.

   D None of the light bulbs will light.

3. **Which of the following changes electrical energy into energy of motion?**

   A motor

   B wind farm

   C electromagnet

   D generator

4. **Which of the following is a true statement about energy?**

   A Energy is always destroyed when a change occurs.

   B Energy is sometimes destroyed when a change occurs.

   C Energy is never destroyed when a change occurs.

   D Energy is not involved in any type of change.

5. **Why might a light bulb filament get hot when electric current flows through it?**

   A The filament is a good conductor.

   B The filament has high resistance.

   C The filament has thick insulation.

   D The filament is in an open circuit.

Unit A California Standards Practice

6. Which of the following actions will cause an electric current to flow in a coil of copper wire?

   A Move a magnet in and out of the coil.

   B Expose the coil to direct sunlight.

   C Wrap the coil around an iron rod.

   D Heat the coil to a high temperature.

7. What is the relationship between magnetic field and distance from the magnet?

   A Magnetic field increases as distance increases.

   B Magnetic field decreases as distance increases.

   C Magnetic field stays the same as distance increases.

   D Magnetic field is not related to distance.

8. What is the purpose of a fuse in an electric circuit?

   A The fuse causes a short circuit.

   B The fuse supplies electrical energy to the circuit.

   C The fuse prevents too much current from flowing.

   D The fuse directs the current along specific paths.

9. What happens when a balloon with a negative charge is brought close to the surface of a wall?

   A The surface of the wall gets a positive charge.

   B The surface of the wall gets a negative charge.

   C The balloon loses its negative charge.

   D The balloon gets a positive charge.

10. The diagram shows four simple electromagnets.

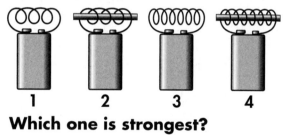

   1   2   3   4

Which one is strongest?

   A 1

   B 2

   C 3

   D 4

Unit A California Standards Practice

11. What causes the metal disc in an earphone to vibrate and make sound?

A An electromagnet produces a magnetic field that changes in strength.

B Electricity moves through the disc and makes a weak electric field.

C Static electricity builds up behind the disc and then is released.

D The disc is attracted to the listener's hair.

12. According to scientists, what might produce Earth's magnetic field?

A Much of Earth's surface is covered with lodestone.

B Earth's solid inner core is a strong magnet.

C Charged particles from space interact with Earth.

D Electric charges flow in Earth's liquid outer core.

13. A man rubs his feet on carpet, and his body becomes charged. Which particles caused this to happen?

A neutral particles

B electrons

C atoms

D drops of water

14. Which of the following is an advantage of parallel circuits over series circuits?

A More resistors can be wired into the circuit.

B Fewer materials and less wire are needed to make the circuit.

C Different appliances can draw different amounts of current.

D Wire that is a poor conductor can be used to make the circuit.

15. What happens if you gently move the two bar magnets in the picture closer together?

A The magnets attract each other.

B The magnets repel each other.

C The magnets do not affect each other.

D One magnet attracts, but the other repels.

Unit A California Standards Practice

16. How can an iron needle be magnetized for a short time?

   A by stroking it in one direction on a permanent magnet

   B by filing it with another piece of iron

   C by rubbing it with a piece of silk cloth

   D by placing the needle in an east-west direction

17. The diagram shows two balloons suspended by string.

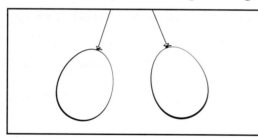

Why do these two balloons repel each other?

   A One balloon has more air in it.

   B Each balloon has a magnetic field.

   C The balloons have unlike electric charges.

   D The balloons have like electric charges.

18. What happens if a bar magnet is broken into two pieces?

   A One piece has two south poles, and one has two north poles.

   B Both pieces have a north pole and a south pole.

   C Neither piece is magnetic.

   D One piece is still magnetic, but the other piece is not.

19. Which of the following is safe to touch?

   A a fallen power line

   B an electric cord with frayed insulation

   C a plastic plug on an electric cord

   D a part inside an electrical outlet

20. Which device is used to open and close a circuit?

   A resistor

   B appliance

   C switch

   D battery

Life Sciences

AVENUE OF THE GIANTS

Northern California

You can see some of the world's tallest trees in Humboldt Redwoods State Park. The park has an area of more than 210 square kilometers. Inside the park, the Avenue of the Giants is more than 50 kilometers of scenic highway. Some redwoods in the park are more than 2,000 years old and more than 90 meters tall! In fact, the park's tallest tree, the Stratosphere Giant, is over 112 meters high. The trunks of these trees are 3 to 6 meters across—wider than a school bus. The trees can grow as much as 2 meters each year. Not far from the Avenue of Giants are three trees with tunnels carved through them. Cars can be driven through the massive trunks!

Humboldt
Redwoods
State Park

Find Out More

Find out more about California's redwood forests. Choose a project to show what you learned.

- Make a poster showing some of the animals and other plants that live in a redwood forest.

- Write a paragraph explaining why it is important to protect California's redwood forests.

- Prepare a multimedia presentation to share facts about the famous General Sherman and General Grant redwood trees, located in Sequoia National Park.

Chapter 3

Flow of Energy and Matter

CALIFORNIA Standards Preview

4LS2.0 All organisms need energy and matter to live and grow. As a basis for understanding this concept:

4LS2.a Students know plants are the primary source of matter and energy in most food chains.

4LS2.b Students know producers and consumers (herbivores, carnivores, omnivores, and decomposers) are related in food chains and food webs and may compete with each other for resources in an ecosystem.

4LS2.c Students know decomposers, including many fungi, insects, and microorganisms, recycle matter from dead plants and animals.

4LS3.0 Living organisms depend on one another and on their environment for survival. As a basis for understanding this concept:

4LS3.d Students know that most microorganisms do not cause disease and that many are beneficial.

4IE6.0 Scientific progress is made by asking meaningful questions and conducting careful investigations. As a basis for understanding this concept and addressing the content of the other three strands, students should develop their own questions and perform their own investigations. (Also **4IE6.a**, **4IE6.f**)

Standards Focus Questions

- How does energy flow?
- How does matter flow?
- What are decomposers?
- What is the role of microorganisms?

How do living things interact in an ecosystem?

ecosystem

producer

herbivore

carnivore

omnivore

DIGITAL

Chapter 3 Vocabulary

consumer

decomposer

microorganism

food chain

food web

91

Lab zone Directed Inquiry

Explore What does an owl eat?

Materials

safety goggles

paper

bone sorting chart

owl pellet and
bone sorting chart

forceps

wooden probe

magnifier

What to Do

1 Place the owl pellet on paper.

2 Separate the bones from the fur
and other material in the pellet.

Be careful!

Be careful while using
sharp objects.

3 Use the bone sorting chart that came with your
owl pellet to help identify the bones. Compare
them to the bones in the chart. List the type
and number of bones you found.

Explain Your Results

What kinds of bones were the most common?
What can you **infer** about the diet of an owl?

Process Skills

Scientists'
explanations come
partly from what
they **observe**
and partly from
the **inferences**
they make
based on their
observations.

4LS2.0 All organisms need energy and matter to live and grow.
4IE6.a Differentiate observations from inference (interpretation) and know
scientists' explanation come partly from what they observe and partly
from how they interpret their observations. **4IE6.f** Follow a set of written
instructions for a scientific investigation.

DIGITAL Lab zone

Follow Instructions

Have you ever read directions to cook or put a toy together? If so, you know that **following instructions** is important.

Some instructions are numbered in order. Others are not. Clues such as *first, next,* and *at the same time* can help you **infer** the order. You read some instructions and listen to others.

Read the letter to the Plant Doctor column of a magazine.

Gardening Magazine Article

Ask the Plant Doctor

Question: I have grown a sweet potato plant in the same place in my yard for ten years. Bushes and trees shade it. This year, the plant looks sickly. I have observed that leaves are drying up and falling off. Some have brown spots with little holes. What is wrong?

Answer: All plants need sunlight, water, and nutrients to make food. Brown spots and holes on leaves are often the result of pests. Follow these instructions to help your plant.

First, trim the trees and bushes. Next, look for harmful pests. Be sure to check the underside of the leaves. Then, add nutrients by mixing fertilizer into the topsoil. Directions on the package will tell you what to do. You may use a garden-safe pest killer at the same time. Water your plant. Gently poke your finger beneath the surface to feel if the soil near the roots is wet. Finally, check daily to see if your plant needs water. Happy growing!

Apply It!
Make a graphic organizer to show how to follow the Plant Doctor's instructions.

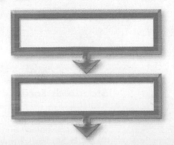

You Are There!

Filtered shade and sunlight dapple the path ahead of you. Ferns and flowering plants line the trail under the cool canopy of the giant redwoods. You stop hiking for a moment to enjoy the stillness of the forest. Instead, you are surprised at the amount of life around you. *Awk! Awk! Squawk!* A bright blue Steller's jay scolds a large black raven, trying to chase it away. The raven complains with a loud *Cawwww!* A chipmunk scurries around the folds of a redwood's trunk. *Shh!* You spy a black-tailed deer, its antlers lit by a beam of sunlight. It is motionless, gazing back at you. Then suddenly it bounds away through the trees. How do these living things depend on each other and their environment?

Standards Focus 4LS2.0 All organisms need energy and matter to live and grow. As a basis for understanding this concept:
4LS2.a Students know plants are the primary source of matter and energy entering most food chains.
4LS2.b Students know producers and consumers (herbivores, carnivores, omnivores, and decomposers) are related in food chains and food webs and may compete with each other for resources in an ecosystem.

DIGITAL

How does energy flow?

Every living thing needs energy. Energy passes from one organism to another.

Energy in Living Things

The redwood forest is one kind of ecosystem. An **ecosystem** is all the living and nonliving things in an environment and the many ways they interact. All living things in an ecosystem need water, nutrients, growing space, and temperatures that allow them to grow and reproduce. Above all, they need energy to survive. They use that energy to grow and for all the processes that keep them alive.

Sources of Energy

But where does the energy in an ecosystem come from? It comes mainly from sunlight. The Sun's energy enters the ecosystem and flows through all the living things. It changes form as it moves through the ecosystem.

The energy flow starts in plants. During the process of *photosynthesis,* green plants use energy from sunlight to change carbon dioxide and water into food and oxygen. Energy that living things can use is stored in food. Plants use the energy from the food they make to grow and live. Some of the energy is stored in parts of the plant such as roots, leaves, and fruits. Plants are called **producers** because they make, or produce, their own food. In almost all ecosystems, green plants are the only producers.

1. ✔Checkpoint What type of living things produce their own food from sunlight?

2. ✏ **Writing in Science Descriptive**
Write a paragraph describing how energy flows into plants and is stored there.

How Energy Flows

Can you make your own food like a plant? No, and neither can any other animal. Animals get energy by eating, or consuming, plants or other animals. Living things that eat other living things are called **consumers**.

The Sun's energy stored in plants flows into the animals that eat the plants. **Herbivores** are animals that eat plants. Each herbivore uses some energy to live and grow. Some energy is released as heat. But some energy is stored in its body. The unused, stored energy is transferred when the herbivore is eaten.

Animals that get food by eating other animals are **carnivores**. The carnivore uses some of the transferred energy to live and grow. The unused energy is stored in the carnivore's body. When the carnivore is eaten, whatever stored energy is left is passed on. Some animals, called **omnivores**, eat plants and other animals. Humans are omnivores. *Scavengers* are consumers that eat dead or decaying plants or animals.

When plants and animals die or leave wastes, what happens to their unused energy? Other organisms such as some insects, fungi, and bacteria break down the dead material or the wastes. The unused energy is transferred to them. Organisms that break down plant and animal waste and remains are called **decomposers**. In this way, energy flows from the Sun, to producers, to consumers, and to decomposers.

A turkey vulture is a scavenger. It feeds mostly on dead and decaying animal matter.

Consumers in the Mojave Desert Ecosystem

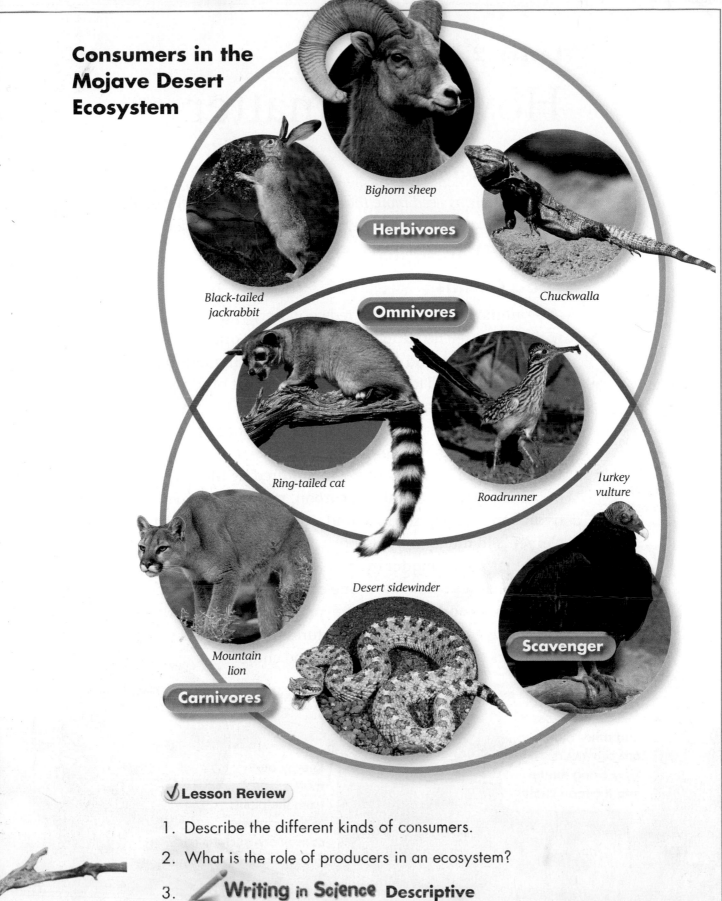

Bighorn sheep

Herbivores

Black-tailed jackrabbit

Chuckwalla

Omnivores

Ring-tailed cat

Roadrunner

Turkey vulture

Mountain lion

Desert sidewinder

Scavenger

Carnivores

✓ Lesson Review

1. Describe the different kinds of consumers.

2. What is the role of producers in an ecosystem?

3. ✏ **Writing in Science Descriptive**
   Describe what would happen to the organisms in an ecosystem if there were no sunlight.

How does matter flow?

All organisms need more than energy to survive. They also need matter in the form of nutrients, oxygen, or carbon dioxide. Energy and matter are passed from one organism to another.

Food Chains

Standing at the base of a redwood tree, you are amazed. Even with arms stretched and hands joined, you and your fellow hikers cannot reach around its trunk. How did such a living thing grow so big? A redwood forest has a huge amount of *biomass,* or mass of living matter. In the redwood forest—and in almost any other ecosystem—plants use the energy in sunlight to produce all of the biomass that other living things need.

You've seen that sunlight gets captured by the green parts of plants. Plants also take in carbon, nitrogen, oxygen, and hydrogen from the soil, air, and water. The plant uses these elements to make its living parts. When animals eat plants, both energy and matter are passed to other living things.

The pictures below show one example of a simple food chain. In a **food chain**, organisms transfer energy by eating and being eaten. Look at the pictures and then identify the producers and consumers in this food chain.

Energy enters the food chain as sunlight that will be used by plants.

Meadow grasses and other plants are producers. They bring matter into the food chain.

Energy and matter flow from the plants to the primary consumers, such as mice.

Standards Focus 4LS2.0 All organisms need energy and matter to live and grow. As a basis for understanding this concept:

4LS2.b Students know producers and consumers (herbivores, carnivores, omnivores, and decomposers) are related in food chains and food webs and may compete with each other for resources in an ecosystem.

4LS2.c Students know decomposers, including many fungi, insects, and microorganisms, recycle matter from dead plants and animals.

Links in a Food Chain

A producer is always the first link in a food chain. In almost all ecosystems, the producer is a plant. In a redwood forest, plants such as rhododendrons, ferns, and mosses may grow between the trees. Grasses may grow in clearings. In the food chain in the pictures, the grasses are the producers.

Mice and golden eagles are also in this food chain. Mice eat the seeds of the grasses. The mice are first or *primary* consumers in the food chain. The mice gain energy and matter from the grasses. The golden eagle is a predator of mice. A *predator* is an animal that hunts other animals for food. The hunted animals are called *prey*. The golden eagle gets its energy and matter from eating mice and other prey.

Food chains may have more than one level of consumers. In this example, the golden eagle is at the top of the food chain. Animals at the top of a food chain have few, if any, predators.

Golden eagles are secondary consumers. They eat mice. Energy and matter flow from the mice to the eagles.

1. **✓ Checkpoint** How does matter flow through an ecosystem?

2. **Follow Instructions** Deer mice are primary consumers, and barn owls are at the top of one food chain. Write instructions that a classmate can follow to draw this food chain.

Food Webs

Most ecosystems are more complicated than what you've read about so far. A Douglas squirrel in a redwood forest eats more than one food. It mostly eats seeds from the redwood cones, but it may also eat acorns, berries, fruits, and mushrooms. The Douglas squirrel must also watch out for more than one type of predator. Its predators include owls and bobcats.

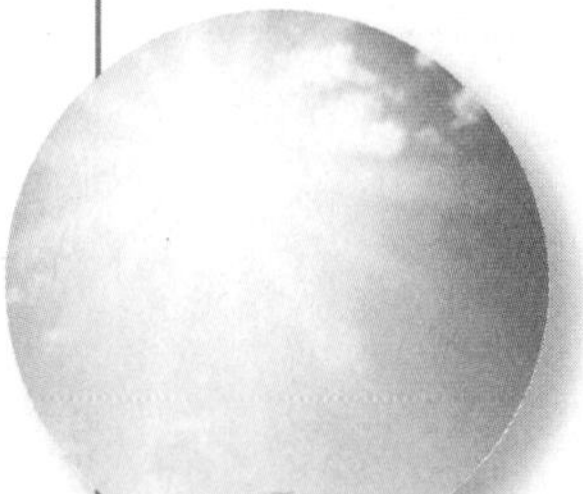

As you can see, many food chains overlap and connect in an ecosystem. A **food web** is a system of overlapping food chains. In a food web, energy and matter can flow through many branches. Look at the pictures on these pages. Trace as many food chains as you can.

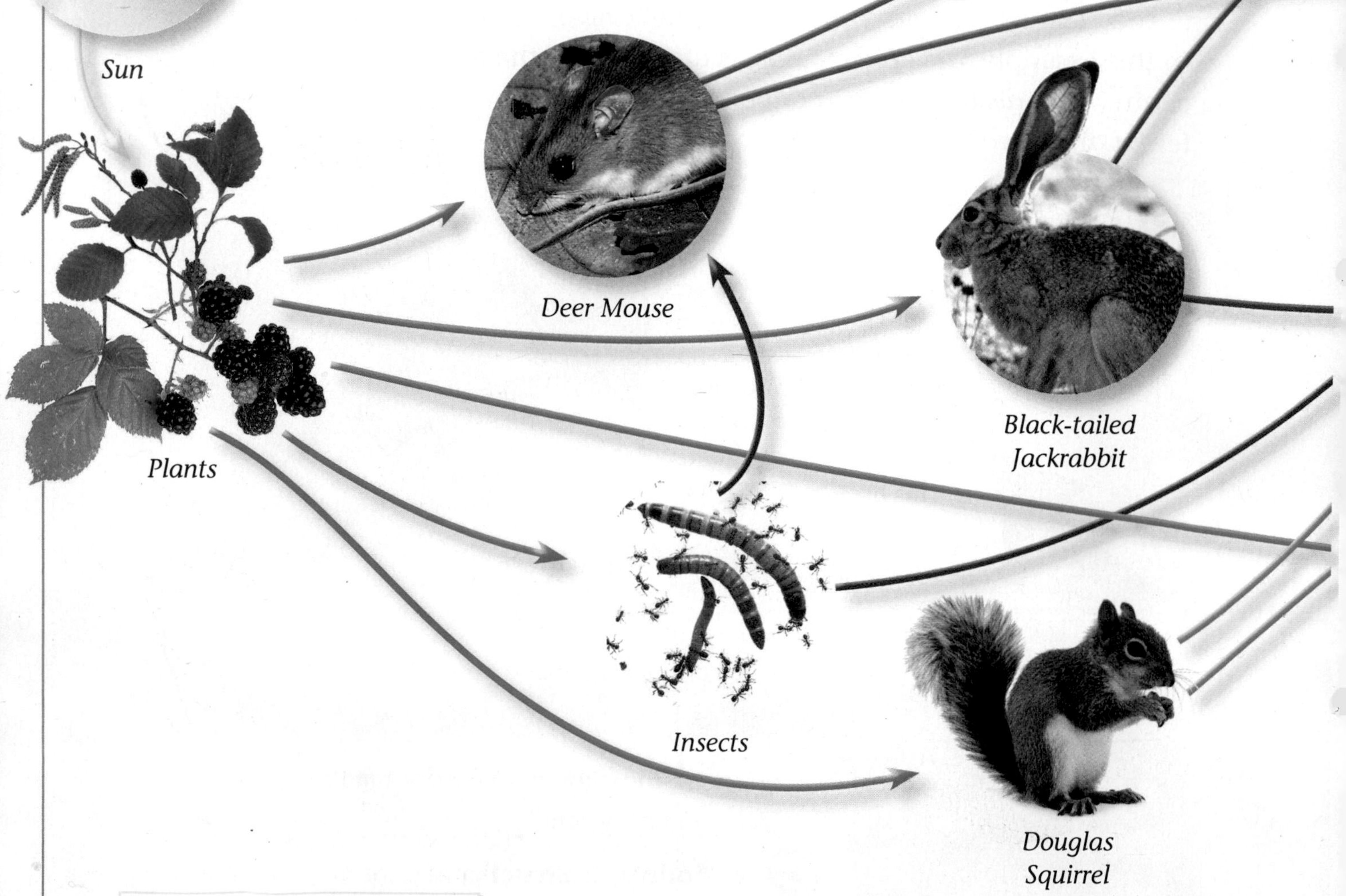

Sun
Deer Mouse
Black-tailed Jackrabbit
Plants
Insects
Douglas Squirrel

DIGITAL Look for Active Art animations at www.pearsonsuccessnet.com

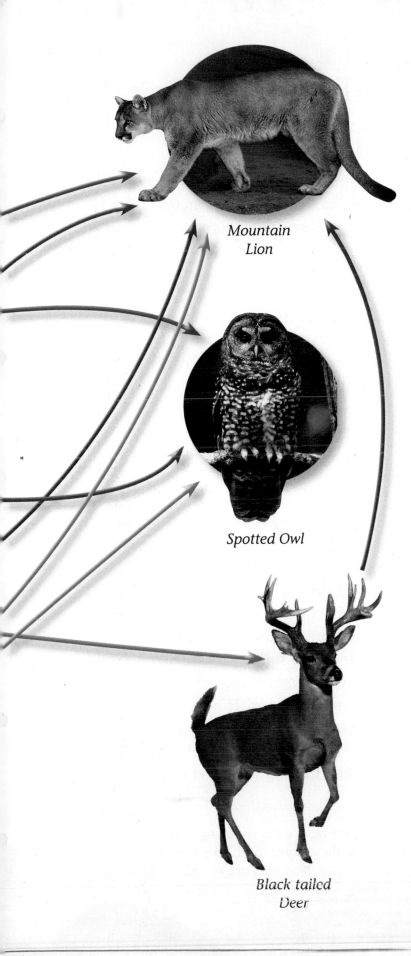

Mountain
Lion

Spotted Owl

Black tailed
Deer

What's Missing

One important part of this food web is not shown. Decomposers such as fungi and bacteria are at each level of the food web. They get what they need from dead organisms and other wastes. Decomposers return matter to the soil and air. Producers can use this matter. You will read more about decomposers in Lesson 3.

Changing Food Webs

What would happen if the number of mountain lions dropped dramatically? Follow each arrow backward from the mountain lion to its prey. With fewer mountain lions to eat them, more jackrabbits, deer mice, Douglas squirrels, and black-tailed deer would survive.

More herbivores would mean more available food for the spotted owls. More herbivores would also mean more plants would get eaten. The number of plants would decrease. This would mean less food for the herbivores, and soon their populations would start to decrease.

All living things are connected in some way. A change in one part of a food web can affect all parts. All living things depend on other living things for what they need to survive.

✓ Lesson Review

1. Give an example of how changing one part of a food web can change other parts of the web.

2. How is a food web different from a food chain?

Lesson 3

What are decomposers?

Decomposers recycle matter from dead plants and animals. Fungi, bacteria, and insects help decompose matter. Many decomposers are too small to see with just your eyes.

The Role of Decomposers

When you think of organisms in an ecosystem, you probably think of the producers and consumers. But there's another important part: decomposers. Without decomposers, plants would use up all the nutrients in the soil. Without the nutrients, plants would die. Then herbivores would die off, too, and the carnivores that eat them would have no food.

Decomposers break down wastes and dead plant and animal material. This material still has food energy stored in it. Decomposers use this energy. As they break down wastes, they release nutrients into the soil and water. Other living things use these nutrients, and the cycle starts again.

Look at the picture of the decomposing saguaro cactus. Caterpillars bore holes in the saguaro, bringing bacteria with them. The bacteria break down the flesh of the cactus. Nutrients return to the soil and are taken up by new saguaro plants. Desert rabbits and other animals eat the tender young saguaro seedlings. Hawks and coyotes hunt the smaller animals, and the cycle continues. Producers keep using energy from the Sun. Decomposers help to recycle the matter through the food web.

Bacteria and other decomposers are breaking down this saguaro cactus.

Earthworms eat decaying matter in the soil. As they digest food, they help decompose matter. Nutrients are released into the soil.

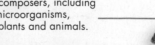

Standards Focus 4LS2.0 All organisms need energy and matter to live and grow. As a basis for understanding this concept: **4LS2.c** Students know decomposers, including many fungi, insects, and microorganisms, recycle matter from dead plants and animals.

Recycling Dead Matter

Ecosystems have limited resources. Living things compete for water, food, light, and space. By consuming dead plants and animals, decomposers add usable resources to the air and soil. At the same time, new space for living things replaces the dead and decaying matter.

Wood rot can start when the bark of a tree is damaged. Tiny organisms enter the wound and multiply. They damage the wood tissue. This change shows as a stain or discolored area in the wood. Fungi and bacteria grow and cause decay.

These tree fungi are called conks. The fungus starts inside the tree. When you see conks growing from the side of a tree, you can infer that the tree is rotting and there is fungus inside.

1. ✔️**Checkpoint** Why are decomposers important in a food web?

2. What are some signs that decomposers are breaking down the saguaro cactus in the photo on page 102?

Types of Decomposers

Have you ever seen a brown spot on a ripe peach? If you left it for a few days, the brown spot would get larger. Decomposers, such as fungi and bacteria, cause these spots as they break down the peach.

Some decomposers are large enough for you to see. But many decomposers are microorganisms. A **microorganism** is a living thing too small to see without a microscope. Bacteria and some fungi are microorganisms.

Microorganisms may be eaten by worms and small insects that help decompose matter. The worms and insects may be eaten by even larger consumers such as birds. The picture below shows some examples of what you might find on a dead log.

Several different types of living things are helping decompose the fallen log.

A fungus breaks down matter by releasing special chemicals. Then the fungus takes in the materials. You may be able to see only part of a fungus. The rest of it is underground or out of sight.

With its yellow coloring and long body, you can see why this is called the banana slug. It eats material on the forest floor. It can grow to be 25 centimeters long.

Decay in Ecosystems

Rot, or decay, is very important to the health of an ecosystem. If nothing decayed, dead organisms and wastes would pile up and interfere with the habitats of living things. Nutrients would not be recycled.

Warm temperatures, oxygen, and moisture all speed up the process of decay. Many insects and worms are scavengers that help the decaying process too. These scavengers feed on the remains of dead organisms. Then decomposers, such as fungi and bacteria, break down whatever is left and return the nutrients to the ecosystem.

✓ Lesson Review

1. Name two different types of decomposers.

2. Why do organisms decay more quickly in the summer than in the winter?

3. **Writing in Science** **Descriptive** How does a scavenger help decompose matter?

Carpenter ants do not eat wood, but they do chew through it to make their homes. The resulting dust of wood particles can be broken down and added to the soil faster than larger pieces of wood.

The almond-scented millipede eats pine needles and other leaves that have fallen from trees.

Slime molds on the log not only decompose matter, but they may eat bacteria as well.

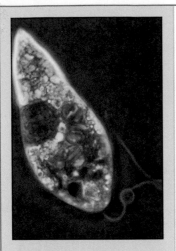

Euglena

Euglena is a special one-celled organism. It is found in ponds and lakes. A whip-like structure attached to one end helps the euglena move. Protists such as euglena are producers. But if sunlight is not available for photosynthesis to take place, the euglena can take in food from its environment.

What is the role of microorganisms?

Many microorganisms have vital roles in food chains as decomposers. Many others are producers. They are also found in some foods and inside the bodies of animals. Microorganisms are used to make medicines and other products.

Microorganisms

Don't look now, but microorganisms are all around you. They're in the air, soil, and water. Some are even on your skin and inside your body! But don't worry. Most of them are harmless. Many microorganisms carry out roles that are helpful and even vital, or necessary, to other living things.

You might be surprised that these tiny life forms far outnumber the plants and animals that are easier to see. A liter of pond or ocean water may contain tens of thousands of tiny floating organisms called protists! Most protists have only one cell. Some, such as algae, are producers. These protists that make their own food are the base of most food webs in Earth's waters. They are the main producers of food in the oceans and in freshwater ecosystems. Other protists help clean the water supply by eating other microorganisms.

Radiolaria are tiny protists with hard outer skeletons. They are consumers. They float in the sea and are eaten by larger protists or animals. When they decompose, their skeletons fall to the seafloor.

Diatoms are microorganisms with hard cell walls. The cell walls form many beautiful shapes and patterns. Diatoms are producers.

Standards Focus 4LS3.0 Living organisms depend on one another and on their environment for survival. As a basis for understanding this concept: **4LS3.d** Students know that most microorganisms do not cause disease and that many are beneficial.

Other Helpful Microorganisms

Helpful microorganisms are found in many places—including inside your digestive system! Bacteria in your intestines not only help digest food, they also crowd out harmful bacteria. You can get these helpful bacteria by eating certain dairy products, such as yogurt, sour cream, buttermilk, and cheese. Cows, buffalo, and other herbivores have bacteria and other microorganisms in their stomachs and intestines that help them digest grass and other plants.

Have you ever seen blue-green mold growing on a decaying orange or lemon? Some of these blue-green molds are fungi called *Penicillium* molds. Scottish scientist Alexander Fleming discovered in 1928 that *Penicillium* mold produces an antibiotic. An antibiotic is a substance that kills disease-causing bacteria. Since then, penicillin and other antibiotics have been used as medicines. Other types of *Penicillium* are used to make certain kinds of cheese.

This picture shows the ropey, beaded structure of the *Pencillium* fungus. The round areas ripen and release spores. Each spore can grow into a new fungus.

Cultured Dairy Products
The sharp or sour flavor of cheese and yogurt comes from helpful bacteria and fungi.

Cultured buttermilk gets its tangy taste from acid these bacteria produce.

Yogurt and buttermilk may have billions of bacteria. These bacteria can live in the intestines and help protect humans from harmful bacteria.

The fungus *Penicillium candidum* gives some cheese its flavor and soft texture. Cheesemakers put the mold into cheese. The mold grows and spreads as the cheese ages.

1. ✓ **Checkpoint** Why are protists important in ocean and freshwater ecosystems?

2. ✏ **Writing in Science** Summarize
How are microorganisms helpful to humans and other living things?

Microorganisms at Work

Good fertile soil is alive! As you can see from the picture below, soil is full of insects and microorganisms. Just one liter-sized lump of dirt can contain up to 1 trillion bacteria, thousands of worms, and 10 to 100 million protists.

Some bacteria in the soil are factories that produce natural plant fertilizer. They change the element nitrogen into a compound that plants can use for growth. Plants also store nitrogen as food in the form of proteins. Proteins are an important part of your diet. All living things need proteins.

Topsoil is teeming with billions and billions of microorganisms and other living things. See how many different kinds you can identify.

Nematodes, or roundworms, live in all types of soil. They feed on decaying matter, bacteria, fungi, or algae.

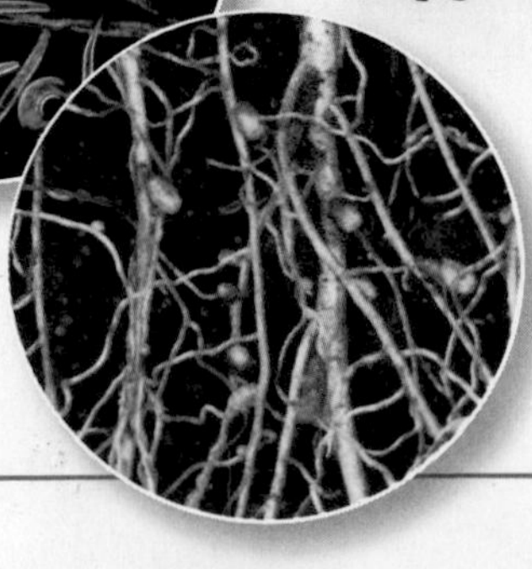

Ants and earthworms are in soil. Centipedes, wood lice, millipedes, and spiders are other soil-dwellers that help decompose matter.

Observing Microorganisms

You can't see microorganisms with just your eyes, but you can find them with a microscope. A mixture of hay, pond water, and distilled water is a good place for microorganisms to grow.

Hay or dried grass is mixed with equal parts of pond water and distilled water. The mixture is kept in the dark at room temperature. After a few days, an eyedropper is used to take a sample of the mixture. The sample might contain some of the microorganisms shown on this page. If the mixture is kept in the dark even longer, more kinds of microorganisms may appear.

Weeks 1–2: Small protists such as these may multiply and then disappear.

Weeks 2–4: Medium-size protists shaped like this one may appear and then die off.

Weeks 3–6: Different kinds of medium-size protists and bacteria may appear.

✓ Lesson Review

1. List two possible roles of microorganisms. Give an example of each.

2. Why are bacteria that change the form of nitrogen important?

3. **Follow Instructions** Suppose you work for a company that sells kits for hay-and-pond water demonstrations. All of the supplies that the customer needs are in the kit. Write instructions that the customer should follow to use the kit.

Recycling a Fraction

Since 1990, Americans have thrown out about 2 kg of garbage per day for every person in the country. That's about 56 kg per week for a family of 4! This garbage doesn't just disappear. Most of it is buried in landfills, and some of it is burned. A fraction of it is recycled. The pictures below show how this fraction has changed, as recycling has become more popular with Americans.

Recycled

Landfill or Burned

What fraction of the garbage was recycled in 1990?

The picture for 1990 shows 6 equal parts.

One part represents the recycled garbage.

$$\frac{1}{6}$$

$1 \leftarrow$ One part is recycled

$6 \leftarrow$ Six equal parts in all

In 1990, $\frac{1}{6}$ of the garbage was recycled.

1990   1995   2000

DIGITAL

Use the pictures on page 110 to answer the questions.

1. In 1995, what fraction of the garbage was recycled?

   A. $\frac{1}{4}$ B. $\frac{1}{3}$ C. $\frac{1}{2}$ D. $\frac{3}{4}$

2. In 1995, what fraction of the garbage was put into landfills or burned?

   A. $\frac{1}{4}$ B. $\frac{1}{3}$ C. $\frac{1}{2}$ D. $\frac{3}{4}$

3. In 2000, what fraction of the garbage was recycled?

   A. $\frac{7}{10}$ B. $\frac{3}{10}$ C. $\frac{1}{3}$ D. $\frac{1}{7}$

4. In 2000, what fraction of the garbage was put into landfills or burned?

   A. $\frac{7}{10}$ B. $\frac{3}{7}$ C. $\frac{3}{10}$ D. $\frac{7}{3}$

5. About how much garbage (in kg) does a family of 8 throw out each day? In 1995, how much of this garbage (in kg) was recycled? Remember: $\frac{1}{4}$ of $n = n \div 4$

Lab zone Take-Home Activity

Find out how much garbage your family would throw out in a day, in a week, and in a year at the rate of 2 kg per person per day. Find how many kilograms of garbage would be recycled in one year if your family members recycled $\frac{1}{10}$ of their garbage.

Investigate How can you show that mold needs food?

Be careful!

Wear gloves.

Materials

gloves

moldy strawberry

magnifier

bread slice (without preservatives)

foil square

2 plastic bags

dropper

cup with water

Process Skills

Accurate **observations** are an important part of a careful **investigation.**

What to Do

1 **Observe** the mold on the strawberry.

Mold, a type of fungi, are decomposers.

2 Lightly rub some mold off the strawberry onto the bread. Do the same for the foil.

4LS2.c Students know decomposers, including many fungi, insects, and microorganisms, recycle matter from dead plants and animals. **4IE6.0** Scientific progress is made by asking meaningful questions and conducting careful investigations. As a basis for understanding this concept and addressing the content in the other three strands, students should develop their own questions and perform investigations. **4IE6.f** Follow a set of written instructions for a scientific investigation.

3 Place the bread in a bag. Put the foil in another bag. Use a dropper to put 10 drops of water on the 2 places where the mold was rubbed.

4 Seal the bags. Put them in a warm, dark place.

Be careful!

After you seal the bags, do not reopen them!

5 After 4 to 6 days, observe your bags. **Observe** the bags of other groups. Draw pictures of any mold growing in the bags.

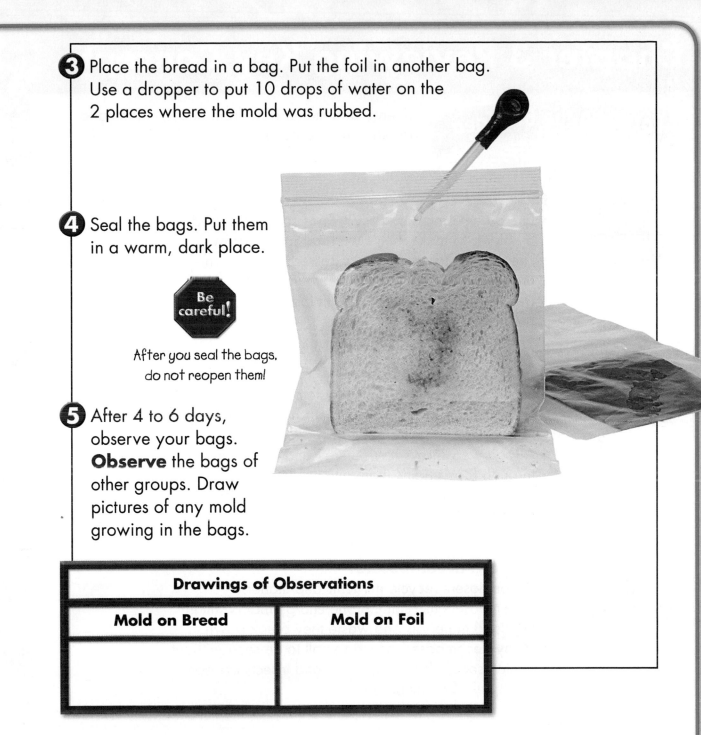

Drawings of Observations	
Mold on Bread	**Mold on Foil**

Explain Your Results

Look at your drawings of the bread and foil. Which can the mold use for food? Explain your answer using your **observations.**

Go Further

How might a lack of moisture affect mold growth? Perform a careful investigation to answer this question or develop a meaningful question of your own.

Chapter 3 Reviewing Key Concepts

Focus on the BIG Idea Energy and matter flow from one living thing to another in an ecosystem.

Lesson 1

How does energy flow?
- Energy entering the ecosystem as sunlight is used by plants to make their own food and to grow.
- The plant's stored energy is passed along to an organism that eats the plant.
- Decomposers use the energy in the wastes they break down.

Lesson 2

How does matter flow?
- Matter is recycled in an ecosystem.
- A food chain shows how matter and energy flow from producers to consumers in an ecosystem.
- A food web shows how energy and matter flow through food chains that have organisms in common.
- Any change to one part of a food web affects other parts too.

Lesson 3

What are decomposers?
- Decomposers recycle nutrients and matter.
- Decomposers use some of the energy that is still in the dead materials and waste they break down.
- Many decomposers are too small to be seen without a microscope. Bacteria, fungi, and insects are some examples of decomposers.

Lesson 4

What is the role of microorganisms?
- Some microorganisms are decomposers.
- Microorganisms that make their own food are the main producers in most water ecosystems.
- Some microorganisms are used to make foods and medicines.
- Microorganisms are in the air, soil, and water, on your skin, and inside your body.

Cross-Curricular Links

English–Language Arts

Building Vocabulary

Look again at pages 90–91. Write a paragraph about the vocabulary term **producer**. Explain in your paragraph how the term is related to the picture that is behind it.

Mathematics

Symmetry

Look again at the pictures of microorganisms on page 106. Which have bilateral symmetry? Which have rotational symmetry? Draw an example of each type.

Health

Microorganisms and Food

Use the library-media center or other resources to find how microorganisms are used to make a variety of tasty foods such as yogurt, cheese, or pickles. Write a report that describes what you find.

Challenge!

Visual and Performing Arts

Fungi

Do research to find the everyday names of different types of fungi. Then choose one type to learn more about. Make a poster to share information such as what that fungus looks like, where it grows best, and other interesting facts.

Use Vocabulary

carnivore (p. 96)	food web (p. 100)
consumer (p. 96)	herbivore (p. 96)
decomposer (p. 96)	microorganism (p. 104)
ecosystem (p. 95)	omnivore (p. 96)
food chain (p. 98)	producer (p. 95)

Fill in the blanks with the correct vocabulary terms. If you have trouble answering a question, read the listed page again.

1. A(n) _____ is a living thing that must eat food to get energy.

2. A(n) _____ makes its own food.

3. A(n) _____ eats plants and animals.

4. A(n) _____ breaks down the wastes and the remains of living things.

5. A(n) _____ shows the flow of energy and matter in an ecosystem from a producer to one or more consumers.

6. A(n) _____ is all the living and nonliving things in an area and the ways they interact.

7. A(n) _____ shows that the flow of energy in an ecosystem branches out through many paths.

Think About It

8. Not all living things eat plants, but almost all living things depend on plants for their energy. Explain why this is true.

9. How does a food web show that the living things in an ecosystem must share available resources?

10. **Process Skills** **Predict** In a garden, caterpillars that eat the leaves of plants are eaten by beetles. What would happen to the population of plants if the beetle population decreased?

11. **Follow Instructions** You have all the supplies to make a model of a food web in a land ecosystem. Make a graphic organizer with instructions to follow for your model.

12. **Writing in Science**

Narrative Suppose your city plans to build a mall in the middle of a forest preserve. Write a letter to your city council representative explaining how building the mall might affect food webs in that forest ecosystem.

California Standards Practice

Write the letter of the correct answer.

13. Which eats only animals?

   A carnivore

   B herbivore

   C omnivore

   D producer

14. Which is a producer?

   A bean plant

   B housefly

   C human

   D hummingbird

15. Which statement is true about protists that make their own food?

   A They are the bacteria that live in the intestines of animals.

   B They change nitrogen so that it can be used by living things.

   C They are the main producers of biomass in water ecosystems.

   D They spread throughout wastes.

16. What is the source of energy in most ecosystems?

   A herbivores

   B decomposers

   C sunlight

   D omnivores

17. Which completes the food chain?

algae → brine shrimp → ? → raccoon

   A hawk

   B marsh grass

   C protist

   D fish

18. Microorganisms are always

   A animals.

   B plants.

   C harmful.

   D very tiny.

19. What can a mixture of hay and water help you do?

   A Identify a meadow food chain.

   B Observe a meadow food web.

   C Classify decomposers.

   D Observe microorganisms.

20. Which are at work recycling the fallen log?

   A omnivores

   B decomposers

   C *Penicillium* mold

   D producers

Rachel Carson

In the 1950s, people used a chemical called DDT to poison harmful insects. Farmers sprayed DDT on their fields. In cities and towns, it was used on the plants in parks.

Rachel Carson was a scientist and a writer. She began to notice that every spring, there were fewer and fewer songbirds. She wondered what was happening to the bird populations. After making careful observations, Carson learned that DDT was building up on land and in lakes and streams. The chemical had entered the food chains and the webs of many ecosystems. For example, a worm would take in DDT from the soil. A robin would then eat the worm. A hawk would eat the robin. Soon, DDT was poisoning the consumers in many food chains.

Through her observations, Carson could see that all of nature is interdependent. She wanted to warn as many people as possible about the dangers of using DDT. In 1962, she wrote a book titled *Silent Spring*. She wanted people to realize that modern technology could destroy habitats and food chains. Almost immediately, laws forbidding the use of DDT were passed. Society has been more aware of ecosystems ever since.

Lab zone Take-Home Activity

Use resources in the library-media center to find information about pesticides that are labeled "garden safe."

Chapter 4
Ecosystems

4LS3.0 Living organisms depend on one another and on their environment for survival. As a basis for understanding this concept:

4LS3.a Students know ecosystems can be characterized by their living and nonliving components.

4IE6.0 Scientific progress is made by asking meaningful questions and conducting careful investigations. As a basis for understanding this concept and addressing the content of the other three strands, students should develop their own questions and perform their own investigations. (Also **4IE6.a**, **4IE6.b**, **4IE6.e**, **4IE6.f**)

Standards Focus Questions

- What are the parts of an ecosystem?

- What are some ecosystems?

How can ecosystems be described?

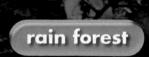
rain forest

climate

desert

DIGITAL

canopy

Chapter 4 Vocabulary

understory

coral reef

symbiosis

Explore What are the living and nonliving parts of a model ecosystem?

Screw cap on tightly!

Materials

2 elodea plants

magnifier

spoon

plastic bottle with water

pond snail

What to Do

1 Put 2 elodea plants in the bottle. Carefully put the pond snail in the bottle. Use a plastic spoon to move the snail.

2 Put the bottle in a bright place but not in direct sunlight.

You should not need to add food, water, or air.

3 **Observe** the snail and elodea each week. Try to observe the snail eating or moving.

Be careful! Wash your hands when finished.

What do the plants need?

What does the snail need?

Explain Your Results

1. Describe the living and nonliving parts of your model ecosystem.

2. What signs of life did you **observe** after a few weeks? **Infer.** Did the plants and snail have what they needed to survive?

3. Explain how your observations and inference are different.

Process Skills

You can use your **observations** to make **inferences.**

DIGITAL Lab zone

4LS3.a Students know ecosystems can be characterized by their living and nonliving components. **4IE6.a** Differentiate observation from inference (interpretation) and know scientists' explanations come partly from what they observe and partly from how they interpret their observations. (Also **4IE6.f**)

How to Read Science

TARGET SKILL Predict

When you predict, you make a statement about what you think might happen in a story, come next in an article, or be the outcome of an experiment. The statement you make is a **prediction**.

- To make a prediction, you can look ahead and get clues from the pictures, titles, topic sentences, and key words. Use what you know to help **infer** what will come next.

- After you make a prediction, keep reading. Check your prediction. As you learn new information, you might need to change your prediction.

Science Article

Habitats

All plants and animals live in a habitat. The ocean is a habitat not only for fish, but also for many other types of animals, and for plants and other organisms. Forests are habitats for foxes, squirrels, birds, and other animals. Sometimes habitats become polluted or destroyed, which can have a damaging effect on the plants and animals living there.

Apply It!

Make a graphic organizer like the one below. Use the information in the article to make a **prediction**.

Information		Prediction
Habitats can become polluted or destroyed.		

You Are There!

The Sun begins to set, giving the dry
landscape an orange glow. Taking care to avoid
cactus spines and rocks, you walk along a dusty trail.
You notice a woodpecker flying to and from its nest in
a towering cactus. A roadrunner on the path ahead stops
for a moment, cocks its head to the side, and stares at you. It
runs away quickly, its feet tapping along the ground. A flash of
movement catches your eye as a black-tailed jackrabbit disappears
into the brush. You hear a coyote yipping in the distance. How can
a harsh, dry land such as this be so full of life?

Standard Focus 4LS3.0 Living organisms depend on one another and on their environment for
survival. As a basis for understanding this concept:
4LS3.a Students know ecosystems can be characterized by their living and nonliving components.

What are the parts of an ecosystem?

An ecosystem is made of living and nonliving parts that all work together. Every organism in an ecosystem has a part to play.

What a System Is

A system is made of many parts that work together for a purpose. A system can have living and nonliving parts. Each part is important. If a part is missing or damaged, the system will not work as well. When you ride a bicycle, the handlebars, pedals, gears, frame, and you work together. Parts of the system interact with other parts. For example, parts attached to the pedals and handlebars allow you to control the speed, brakes, and gears.

Nonliving and Living Parts of an Ecosystem

An ecosystem is one kind of system. An ecosystem is all of the living and nonliving things in an environment and the many ways they interact. An ecosystem may be as large as a desert or as small as a rotting cactus.

Animals, plants, fungi, protists, and bacteria are the living parts of an ecosystem. These organisms interact with one another and with the nonliving parts of the system. The nonliving parts of an ecosystem include air, water, soil, light, temperature, landforms, and climate. **Climate** is the average weather conditions in an area over a long period of time.

1. **✓ Checkpoint** What are some nonliving parts of an ecosystem?

2. **Writing in Science Descriptive** Give an example of a system from your everyday life. Describe how the parts work together.

Nonliving Parts Affect Living Parts

Organisms survive only in environments where their needs are met. In any environment, some kinds of plants and animals will survive better than others. Some will not survive at all. Soil, water, air, light, temperature, and climate determine what kinds of organisms can live in an ecosystem.

For example, a desert is very dry with little water. It may be very hot too. Plants and animals that do well there have body structures that help them conserve water and stay cool. The stem of a giant saguaro cactus can expand to fill up with water. It can store plenty of water until the next rainfall. You will read more about deserts in Lesson 2.

The pictures on these pages show several types of ecosystems. Think about how the nonliving parts of each ecosystem affect which animals and plants can live there.

River
Water moss, duckweed, algae, insects, fish, frogs, and birds are some living parts of river ecosystems. Most organisms live in areas where the water moves slowly. They live in pools or sheltered areas such as under rocks.

Grassland
A grassland, as its name suggests, is covered with grasses. Flowering plants may also grow there. Grasslands receive a medium amount of rain. Grasshoppers, hawks, and deer are some animals that live in the grasslands of North America.

DIGITAL Look for Active Art animations at www.pearsonsuccessnet.com

Tundra

A tundra is a cold, dry region. The ground beneath the surface is frozen all year long. Some grasses and other plants can grow in a tundra, but trees cannot grow. Arctic foxes, caribou, and other animals live in these areas.

Swamp

A swamp is a kind of wetland. Wetlands are places where the ground is covered with water for at least part of the year. Water lilies, vines, and cypress trees grow in some swamps. Different kinds of animals, such as insects, water birds, and alligators live in swamps.

✓ Lesson Review

1. List the living and nonliving parts of three ecosystems.

2. How do the nonliving parts of a tundra ecosystem influence its plant life?

3. **Predict** How might a swamp change if very little precipitation falls on the area for several years?

Lesson 2

What are some ecosystems?

California has high desert and low desert ecosystems. Rain forests and coral reefs are other examples of ecosystems.

Desert

When someone says "desert," what do you think of? Do you picture blowing sand and cactus plants? A **desert** is an ecosystem that receives very little precipitation, usually less than 25 centimeters in a year.

Deserts have nonliving parts that can be very different. Many deserts are hot, but they can be much cooler at night. Some can be quite cold much of the time. Some deserts have sand dunes, and some are mountainous and rocky.

Desert Life

Desert plants have special structures that help them survive in the dry conditions. Some desert plants have large root systems that spread out near the surface of the ground. This allows the roots to take up any rainwater quickly. Many desert plants are shrubs or bushes. A *shrub* is a woody plant that does not have a single trunk like a tree. It usually has branches that spread out from its base.

Animals are adapted to desert conditions too. Because of the high temperatures, many animals rest during the day. They are more active when temperatures are cooler. They often hunt for food at dawn or dusk or when it is completely dark.

Colorado Desert

Map Fact

The Colorado Desert in the southern part of California is a low desert. It is part of the Sonoran Desert that extends into California from Mexico and Arizona.

Standards Focus 4LS3.0 Living organisms depend on one another and on their environment for survival. As a basis for understanding this concept: **4LS3.a** Students know ecosystems can be characterized by their living and nonliving components.

The Low Desert

California has low desert and high desert regions. The Colorado Desert in southern California is less than 915 meters above sea level. Some areas are more than 71 meters below sea level!

Landforms in the low desert include flat, sandy areas, salt flats, and low mountains. The low desert gets 5–15 centimeters of water per year. Sometimes rain comes in sudden strong downpours that can cause floods.

Ocotillo and creosote shrubs grow in the low desert, along with cholla cactus. Animals such as bighorn sheep, bobcats, ground squirrels, lizards, and birds make their homes among these plants.

The High Desert

The Mojave Desert is California's high desert region. It gets very hot in summer but during the winter, snow may fall! The high desert has mountains, hills of sand, and flat areas. Some of it is covered in salt. Most of the high desert ranges from about 915 to 3353 meters above sea level, though places in Death Valley are more than 60 meters below sea level. The Mojave gets between 7 and 26 centimeters of water in the form of rain or melted snow each year.

Plants in the high desert include Joshua trees, sagebrush, giant juniper bushes, pinyon pines, and Mojave creosote. Animals such as desert kit foxes, bighorn sheep, coyotes, black-tailed jackrabbits, and kangaroo rats live there too.

Mojave Desert

Map Fact

The Mojave Desert is a high desert region.

1. ✔ **Checkpoint** How are the living and nonliving parts of high and low deserts different?

2. ✏ **Writing in Science Narrative** Find out more about a state or national park in California's desert regions. Write a report describing what you might see on a visit to the park.

DIGITAL

keyword: desert

code: gr4p128

Tropical Rain Forest

A **rain forest** is any ecosystem that has large amounts of rain and thick plant growth. Most rain forests are tropical. They are near Earth's equator, in regions which are usually hot and humid. Some tropical rain forests get more than three meters of rain every year!

Tropical rain forests have more types of living things than any other land ecosystem. Broad-leaved trees grow tall as they compete for sunlight. Tree branches and leaves tangle together overhead to form the **canopy.** The canopy may be 30–50 meters above ground. It has little or no space between treetops. Most rain forest animals, including kinkajous, brightly colored butterflies and birds such as the toucan, live in the canopy.

Beneath the canopy, shade-loving plants grow in a zone called the **understory**. Small trees, vines, orchids, and ferns grow in the understory. The forest floor is below the understory. The forest floor may be bare or thinly covered with dead and decaying leaves. The ground may be moist or soggy.

Canopy
Animals that live in the canopy may spend their entire lives in the treetops and never go down to the forest floor.

Forest floor
Very little light reaches the forest floor. Only a few bushes and other plants can grow there. Insects, earthworms, fungi, and other decomposers break down plant matter that has fallen from the canopy and understory.

Understory
Some sunlight but few breezes reach the shady, humid understory. Shrubs, small trees, vines, ferns, and flowers grow here. Some vines wrap around the trunks of the taller trees.

Temperate Rain Forest

Other rain forests, such as the one pictured above, are found in temperate areas. *Temperate* means the temperature is not very hot and not very cold. Temperate rain forests are cooler than tropical rain forests. Like tropical rain forests, they get large amounts of rain and are home to many plants and animals. The redwood forests of California's northern coast are part of a temperate rain forest.

1. ✔**Checkpoint** How is a tropical rain forest different from a temperate rain forest?

2. **Predict** Almost all of the nutrients needed by tropical rain forest plants are in the forest's trees and shrubs. The soil has very few nutrients. If plants are cut down completely or burned, how will this affect new plant growth?

A kinkajou will use its tail to help it move through the canopy.

Wet or Dry?

The amount of rain and snow, or precipitation, that falls is an important nonliving part of an ecosystem. A bar graph can help you compare the precipitation in different ecosystems.

The table shows the approximate total precipitation each year at six places in California.

Place	Chico	Death Valley	Fresno	Klamath	Mount Wilson	Sacramento
Precipitation (cm)	65	5	30	200	90	45

Follow these steps to make a bar graph.

1. First, give the graph a title and label the axes. Then, find the range of the data. The data above range from 5 cm to 200 cm. An axis labeled from 0 to 200 will show all of the data.

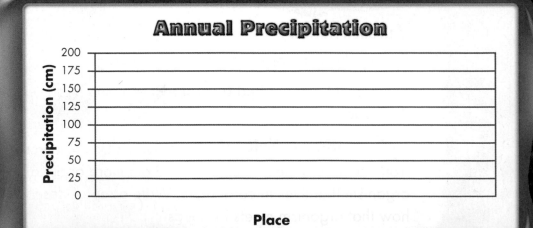

2. Then, draw a bar for each place. For example, find the level that matches the amount of precipitation for Chico. Draw a line at that point, 65 cm. The line will be the top of the bar. Then draw, color, and label the bar.

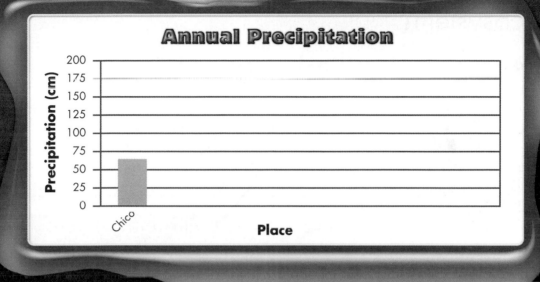

Use the data and the graph to answer each question.

1. Copy the bar graph on grid paper and complete it. Your graph should show the data for all six places.

2. Which place probably has a rain forest ecosystem?

A. Chico

B. Klamath

C. Mount Wilson

D. Sacramento

3. Write a question that you could answer using the information on your graph. Then answer it.

Lab zone Take-Home Activity

Find the monthly precipitation in your area. Show the data in a bar graph.

Investigate What are some common living and nonliving things you can find in your local ecosystem?

Materials

assigned plot area, (1 meter square outlined with string by teacher)

thermometer

2 pieces of string

magnifier

4 index cards

meterstick

Process Skills

Scientific progress is made by asking meaningful questions and conducting careful **investigations.**

What to Do

1 Use 2 strings to divide your plot into 4 squares. **Estimate** and then **measure** the length of each side to make sure they are truly squares. Use index cards to label the squares A, B, C, and D.

1 meter

4LS3.a Students know ecosystems can be characterized by their living and nonliving components. **4IE6.0** Scientific progress is made by asking meaningful questions and conducting careful investigations. As a basis for understanding this concept and addressing the content in the other three strands, students should develop their own questions and perform investigations. **4IE6.b** Measure and estimate the weight, length, or volume of objects. (Also **4IE6.e, 4IE6.f**)

DIGITAL Lab zone

2 Use a magnifier to look for living things in Square A. Record the living things you **observe.**

3 Observe the nonliving parts. Record the things you find. Record the amount of light and moisture. Put a thermometer on the ground. After 3 minutes **measure** and record the temperature.

 Wash your hands when finished.

4 Repeat for each square.

Square	Observations	
	Living Components	**Nonliving Components**
A		
B		

Explain Your Results

1. What living things were in the most squares? Which were the most common?

2. Describe the nonliving parts you observed in your **investigation.**

Go Further

How does the temperature of your plot change? Measure the temperature throughout the day. Show your results on a graph. If you wish, develop your own question about your local ecosystem to investigate.

Chapter 4 Reviewing Key Concepts

An ecosystem can be described by its living and nonliving parts.

Lesson 1

What are the parts of an ecosystem?
- Ecosystems have living and nonliving parts.
- The living parts of an ecosystem include protists, bacteria, fungi, plants, and animals.
- Climate, air, water, and land are some of the nonliving parts.

Lesson 2

What are some ecosystems?
- Deserts, rain forests, grasslands, and tundras are some land ecosystems.
- Deserts get very little precipitation, but they are not always hot.
- Rain forests get a great deal of precipitation. Not all rain forests have warm temperatures all the time.
- Water ecosystems include coral reefs, rivers, and swamps.

Cross-Curricular Links

English–Language Arts

Building Vocabulary

Look again at the picture on page 120. Find the word **climate**. Describe what the picture tells you about the climate in the area where the picture was taken.

Mathematics

Temperature

A ranger records a temperature of −21°C. Explain what this means.

History–Social Science

An Ecosystem in California

Choose a region in California. Use library-media center resources to find more about an ecosystem in the region. Describe the effect of the environment on people's lives. Then describe the effect of human activities such as transportation and the growth of towns on the environment.

Challenge!

English–Language Arts

Deep-Water Coral

Not all corals form reefs in warm, shallow water. Find information about corals that live in deep water. Then write a paragraph or make a poster that describes what the coral looks like, where it lives, what species live near it, and other interesting facts.

Use Vocabulary

canopy (p. 130)	**rain forest** (p. 130)
climate (p. 125)	
coral reef (p. 132)	**symbiosis** (p. 132)
desert (p. 128)	**understory** (p. 130)

Fill in the blanks with the correct vocabulary terms. If you have trouble answering a question, read the listed page again.

1. The top level of a rain forest is called the ____.

2. Less than 25 centimeters of rain or snow falls in a(n) ____ each year.

3. The ____ of an ecosystem is its average weather conditions.

4. Shrubs and vines grow in the ____ of a rain forest ecosystem.

5. A(n) ____ is a ridge or mound formed by the skeletons of tiny marine organisms.

6. The relationship of coral and algae is an example of ____.

Think About It

7. How is an ecosystem a type of system?

8. Some of Earth's tallest trees are in rain forest ecosystems. Why do many trees grow tall in a rain forest?

9. **Process Skills** **Form Questions** List three questions that you might ask to learn more about an ecosystem that you've never studied.

10. **Classify** the following as nonliving or living parts of a swamp ecosystem: temperature, alligator, thunderstorms, warm summers, bald cypress, snails, water level, islands, vines, shrub, water lilies, sandy soil, and bobcat.

11. **Predict** An ecosystem averages 6 centimeters of precipitation each year. The graph shows its monthly average high temperatures.

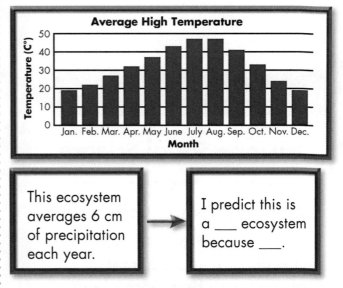

Average High Temperature

This ecosystem averages 6 cm of precipitation each year. → I predict this is a ____ ecosystem because ____.

Copy the graphic organizer. Use what you know to complete the prediction.

12. **Writing in Science**

Descriptive Describe a rain forest ecosystem as if you were there. Include details about sights, sounds, and other things your senses tell you.

California Standards Practice

Write the letter of the correct answer.

13. Trees cannot grow in the frozen soil of which ecosystem?

  A desert

  B grassland

  C temperate rain forest

  D tundra

14. Which words describe an ecosystem's climate?

  A hilly and steep

  B cold and wet

  C rocky cliffs

  D shady and dark

15. Which living things are found in or around a river ecosystem?

  A frogs, dragonflies, fish, birds

  B grasshoppers, mice, lizards, meadowlarks

  C clownfish, algae, clams, anemones

  D coyotes, snakes, jackrabbits

16. Which statement describes temperate rain forests?

  A They are warm and humid all year.

  B They receive the least rainfall of any ecosystem.

  C Only grasses can grow there.

  D They receive a lot of rain but can be warm or cool.

17. A rain forest floor usually has

  A thick, rich soil.

  B dense shrubs.

  C the most animal life.

  D few plants.

18. Most tropical rain forest animals

  A live in the canopy.

  B live in the understory.

  C nest on the forest floor.

  D stay underground.

19. Where can coral reefs form?

  A in ocean water

  B in slow-moving rivers

  C in fast-flowing rivers

  D in swamps

20. Which ecosystem does the picture show?

  A desert

  B grassland

  C redwood forest

  D wetland

Ecosystems in Space

Astronauts need the same things in space that they do on Earth—food, water, and oxygen. None of these things are in space. Astronauts must take enough of these necessities with them to last until they return home.

But what if you want to stay in space for a long time? A space station does not have enough room to store several years' supply of food and water.

In growth chambers, NASA scientists are working to solve this problem. Their goal is to make an ecosystem that can continually recycle energy and matter in space. Plants are being used to create this ecosystem.

Plants provide food. Because the plants keep producing food, less food needs to be stored. Two plants that have been tested are wheat and potatoes. These plants provide some of the nutrition that people need to live.

Plants also help maintain a balance in the air. They take in carbon dioxide and give off oxygen. People breathe in oxygen and give off carbon dioxide. Scientists hope that plants in a space station will create an ecosystem that produces enough oxygen for the astronauts.

Through different processes, plants can purify water. In this way, plants can supply clean water for the astronauts. Scientists still have a lot of work to do before an ecosystem in space is a reality. They will continue to look for answers to the problems of living in space.

Lab zone Take-Home Activity

Scientists know that cattails and certain other plants can improve the quality of water in wetlands on Earth. Use research materials to learn more about cattails, rushes, and other plants that help purify water.

Oceanographer

Evan B. Forde is an oceanographer for the National Oceanic and Atmospheric Administration (NOAA).

Hot springs, or "black smokers," appear near volcanoes on the ocean floor. Black smokers shoot out water that is rich in chemicals. Very unusual forms of life live near black smokers. Some of these living things are not found anywhere else on Earth.

People who study black smokers and other physical features and life forms on the ocean floor are called oceanographers. Actually, oceanographers study many parts of the ocean, not just what's near the bottom. They are concerned with how the living and nonliving parts of the ocean ecosystem interact.

Perhaps you are interested in the tides. Or you may want to know more about the different rocks and minerals found in the sea. You may want to discover new kinds of fish, plants, or other organisms found in the ocean. If so, you can study any of these things by becoming an oceanographer.

Oceanographers also study how hurricanes form. They find ways to detect when hurricanes are just beginning to form so that they can predict where the hurricanes might hit. NASA satellites help them get more information about the ocean.

To prepare to be an oceanographer, learn all you can about life sciences and earth sciences.

Lab zone Take-Home Activity

Scientists need special equipment to explore the ocean floor. Use resources from the library-media center to learn about the special tools that oceanographers use. Write a paragraph about what you find.

Chapter 5
Interactions in Ecosystems

4LS2.0 All organisms need energy and matter to live and grow. As a basis for understanding this concept:

4LS2.b Students know producers and consumers (herbivores, carnivores, omnivores, and decomposers) are related in food chains and food webs and may compete with each other for resources in an ecosystem.

4LS3.0 Living organisms depend on one another and on their environment for survival. As a basis for understanding this concept:

4LS3.b Students know that in a particular environment, some kinds of plants and animals survive well, some survive less well, and some cannot survive at all.

4LS3.c Students know that many plants depend on animals for pollination and seed dispersal, and animals depend on plants for food and shelter.

4IE6.0 Scientific progress is made by asking meaningful questions and conducting careful investigations. As a basis for understanding this concept and addressing the content of the other three strands, students should develop their own questions and perform their own investigations. (Also **4IE6.a**, **4IE6.b**, **4IE6.c**, **4IE6.f**)

Standards Focus Questions

- What determines survival?
- How do environmental changes affect living things?
- How do animals depend on plants?
- How do plants depend on animals?

How do living things survive in an ecosystem?

community

population

DIGITAL g

146

Chapter 5 Vocabulary

competition

adaptation

pollinate

seed dispersal

Explore How does crowding affect plants?

Materials

2 small paper cups

pencil

spoon

potting soil

90 radish seeds

water

What to Do

1. Use a pencil to make 4 small holes in the bottom of each cup. Half-fill each cup with soil.

2. Sprinkle 10 radish seeds in one cup. Sprinkle 80 seeds in the other cup. Cover the seeds in both cups with soil.

   First, think about what might cause a plant to grow better. Next, think about the effects of crowding. Then, make a **prediction.** In which cup will plants survive better? Explain how you made your prediction.

3. Add 5 spoonfuls of water to both cups. Put them in a bright place. Add 1 spoonful of water to each cup daily.

4. Every few days for 3 weeks, observe the plants in each cup. Record their number and appearance.

Label the cups.

Explain Your Results

After 3 weeks in which cup did plants survive better? Compare your results with your **prediction.**

DIGITAL Lab zone

4LS3.b Students know that in any particular environment, some kinds of plants and animals survive well, some survive less well, and some cannot survive at all. **4IE6.c** Formulate and justify predictions based on cause-and-effect relationships. (Also **4IE6.f**)

How to Read Science

Cause and Effect

A **cause** is why something happens. An **effect** is what happens. Sometimes clue words such as *because* and *since* signal a cause and effect. Sometimes there are no clue words, or the author does not tell why something happened. The student who wrote the lab report below could use causes and effects to **predict** what happens when plants grow close together.

Radish Seed Lab Report

Procedure

Day	Procedure	Observations
1	We planted radish seeds in two small milk cartons. We filled each milk carton with garden soil. We planted 3 radish seeds in carton A and 20 radish seeds in carton B.	The cartons are the same size and contain the same amount of soil. The only difference is the number of seeds.
7	We watered the seeds in each carton every two days.	The seeds are sprouting. We see a few plants in carton A. We see more plants in carton B.
20	The plants have been growing for two weeks.	The plants in carton A are tall and full. The plants in carton B are much smaller and look crowded.

Apply It!

Make a graphic organizer like the one at the right. Use it to explain what happened in the carton with more seeds.

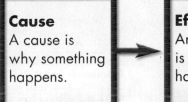

Cause
A cause is why something happens.

Effect
An effect is what happens.

You Are There!

Chirp! Chirp! Ribbit! You are sitting outside on a warm summer night, listening to the musical sounds of crickets and frogs. As you watch and listen, an owl makes a low whoo as it lands on the high branches of a tall pine tree. It turns its head. You can see its face and two huge eyes in the moonlight. Suddenly the owl spreads its white wings and swoops down, talons outstretched. It grabs a mouse that you hadn't even noticed. The interaction between the owl and the mouse is one of many between living things.

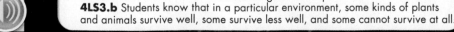

Standards Focus 4LS2.0 All organisms need energy and matter to live and grow. As a basis for understanding this concept:
4LS2.b Students know producers and consumers (herbivores, carnivores, omnivores, and decomposers) are related in food chains and food webs and may compete with each other for resources in an ecosystem.
4LS3.0 Living organisms depend on one another and on their environment for survival. As a basis for understanding this concept:
4LS3.b Students know that in a particular environment, some kinds of plants and animals survive well, some survive less well, and some cannot survive at all.

DIGITAL

Lesson 1

What determines survival?

Living things need food, air, water, and living space to survive. They may have to compete with other living things to get what they need.

Competition

You may have seen only one owl, but more are living nearby. All of these owls make up a population. A **population** is all of the same kind of living things that live in one place. All of the different populations in that place make up a **community**.

Members of a population of animals might work together to hunt. A population might travel together to protect the group from predators. But sometimes the environment might not have enough resources for all the members of the population. **Competition** occurs when two or more living things must use the same limited resources. Owls compete for food, shelter, and places to hunt. Mice compete for food, shelter, and places to hide from owls and other predators.

Plants also compete for resources. Many seedlings might sprout close together. Only a few will become fully-grown plants because there is not enough space for all of them. The taller plants will get more sunlight than the shorter plants will. Through photosynthesis, they will be able to make more food than their shaded neighbors.

Different populations in a community may also compete. Snakes that eat mice may be part of the community. The owls and snakes compete for the same population of mice.

Mistletoe takes water and nutrients from the tree. This is how it competes with other plants to survive.

1. **Checkpoint** List three examples of competition in nature.

2. **Cause and Effect** What causes competition between living things?

 keyword: competition code: gr4p151

151

Sharing Resources

Animals sometimes behave in ways that help reduce competition. For example, both owls and hawks feed on the same kinds of prey. Hawks hunt during the day, but owls hunt at night. This reduces competition while the birds hunt. It helps them share the same food resources.

You read about symbiosis in Chapter 4. Symbiosis can help living things share resources. Lichens, for example, are fungi and algae that live together. The algae use sunlight to make food. The fungi take in some of this food. The fungi protect the algae by giving them a safe home.

Sometimes symbiosis helps one organism but hurts the other. The organism that is helped is called a parasite. The one that is hurt is called a host. The mistletoe that you just saw is a parasite. It takes nutrients and water from the tree, its host.

Bears are omnivores. They eat whatever insects and other foods they find. This bear is licking beetles from a tree.

After sleeping much of the winter, black bears become active in the spring. They eat newly sprouted grasses and other plants.

A Varied Diet

Remember that animals are consumers. They must eat other organisms. Some consumers compete by eating many different kinds of foods. Black bears, for example, eat a variety of foods, depending on what is easy to find.

In spring, bears eat grasses and meadow plants. All summer they claw at logs and stumps looking for insects. In late summer and fall, they eat pine cones, acorns, berries, and nuts that have ripened. They catch fish in streams or the ocean when they can. They will even eat from people's trash cans!

In late summer, salmon return from the ocean to freshwater streams along California's coast. That's when black bears go fishing.

1. ✓ **Checkpoint** What are some ways that animals share resources?

2. How does eating many types of food help a black bear survive in its environment?

153

Claiming and Defending Territory

Have you ever watched red-winged blackbirds defend a nesting area? One bird will chase another bird away. The bird that claims the area will stay near the nest and sing loudly. This bird is defending its *territory*, or area.

Many animals compete for territory. They get food, water, and living space from the territory. Having a territory makes it easier for the animal to get the resources it needs to survive.

Animals use special behaviors to claim and defend their territory. They may also warn others to stay away from it. Male crickets sing loudly and fight each other for territory. Male dragonflies fight each other in the air. Even male butterflies will defend their perching places.

Birds also have many behaviors for claiming or defending territory. They may strut, sing, or spread their wings wide to appear threatening. They may chase or dive at approaching animals. Avocets are long-legged shore birds that work together to protect their nesting areas. They try to distract predators by making loud noises and rushing away from the nest. These behaviors help their population survive.

An avocet spreads its wings. This display is one way that it protects itself from predators.

Red-winged blackbirds have a bright red patch. When defending a territory, the males sing and spread their wings to show the most red.

154

Plants Compete for Resources

Hikers in the desert often notice that creosote plants seem to "claim" a territory where few or no other plants will grow. Creosote plants have a wide, shallow root system that can take in water as soon as it collects on the surface. This prevents other plants from sprouting. Creosote bushes are very successful at competing. Some plants are as old as 11,000 years!

A marsh wren claims its territory by singing loudly day and night.

Mammals also claim and defend territories. Male bighorn sheep, elk, and deer may crash their antlers or horns together to compete for territory and mates. If skunks feel threatened, they spray animals that get too close. The spray smells bad, driving the other animal away.

✓Lesson Review

1. Give three examples of ways living things compete for resources.

2. 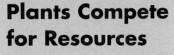 **Writing in Science** **Descriptive**
   Use library-media center or other resources to learn how one kind of animal identifies and defends its territory. Then write a paragraph describing how these behaviors help the animal to survive well in its environment.

Lesson 2

How do environmental changes affect living things?

Environments may change. Plants and animals have adaptations that help them survive when their environment changes.

Ptarmigans are gray or brown in summer.

Ptarmigans are white in winter.

Adaptations for Survival

You would not expect to find a redwood tree in a desert or a desert snake in a tropical rain forest. Many plants and animals survive better in one environment than in another. Living things that survive well have adaptations to their environment. An **adaptation** is a trait that helps a living thing survive in its environment.

For example, white-tailed ptarmigans change color during the year. In the spring, they have gray or brown feathers. These colors help them blend in with the plants where they nest and feed. When winter snows come, the ptarmigans grow white feathers. This color change is an adaptation. The white feathers are harder for predators to see in the snow.

A change in an environment can cause problems for living things. Many birds migrate to salt marshes in California. Over the past 150 years, about nine-tenths of these salt marshes have been built over or drained. There is less space for the migrating birds. The changing environment makes it harder for the birds to survive. Some survive, some don't.

Standards Focus 4LS3.0 Living organisms depend on one another and on their environment for survival. As a basis for understanding this concept:
4LS3.b Students know that in a particular environment, some kinds of plants and animals survive well, some survive less well, and some cannot survive at all.

A whale inhales and exhales at the water's surface through a blowhole on the top of its head.

A whale's smooth skin, flippers, and tail fluke are adaptations that help it swim underwater.

Whales have a layer of fats and oils called blubber. This thick, blubbery skin is an adaptation. It keeps them warm in cold water.

DIGITAL

Look for Active Art animations at www.pearsonsuccessnet.com

Whales' Adaptations

All whales are adapted to breathe, swim, and stay warm in their cold water enviroment. Certain kinds of whales are also adapted to feeding underwater. Baleen whales, such as the humpback whale in the picture, squeeze seawater out of their mouths through plates called baleen. The baleen traps tiny organisms called plankton that are the whale's food. One of the world's largest animals survives by eating tiny sea life!

1. ✔ **Checkpoint** What adaptations help a humpback whale survive in its environment?

2. Give an example of how a change in an environment has affected living things.

How Plants Survive

Like animals, plants have adapted to help them survive. Plants that normally live in a particular environment are usually well adapted to that environment. For example, pine trees have waxy leaves shaped like thin needles. The needles do not lose much water. Some plants have thorns or poisonous leaves for protection from animals.

Flowering plants must be pollinated for seeds to form. **Pollination** is the movement of plant pollen from a male part of a flower to a female part. Birds, bats, and insects pollinate plants when they use the plants for food. Flowers with bright petals and sweet smells are adaptations that attract pollinating animals.

When the weather changes, so do many plants. In winter, many plants stop using sunlight to make food. Their leaves turn brown and drop off. Some plants can store food in their roots or stems. This way, if the environment changes, the plant may survive until it can grow again.

A crimson columbine's petal color, sweet scent, and shape attract pollinators such as hummingbirds.

Coyote mint grows in California's coastal ranges. Its minty smell attracts butterflies.

Skunk cabbage grows in shady, moist forest areas. Its huge leaves help the plant compete for light.

Some plants have thick leaves and stems that store water. This helps them survive in dry areas.

As you have read, plants compete for sunlight, water, soil, nutrients, and living space. In a group of the same kind of plant, some plants will get more nutrients than others. This helps them grow taller. The taller plants will get more sunlight, helping them make more food.

✔ Lesson Review

1. Give three examples of adaptations that help plants survive well during changes in their environment.

2. **Cause and Effect** A population of ferns grows in a shady part of a forest. Some ferns are taller than others, however. What could cause this?

Sundews and pitcher plants live in places where the soil has few nutrients. The plants get nutrients by trapping and digesting insects.

Redwoods

What adaptations help redwoods survive? For one thing, they can sprout directly from a root, a stump, or even the side of a tree. They grow very quickly when conditions are good, but can also survive well when conditions are not good. Their thick bark and high leaves help them resist diseases, insects, and fire. The fog that is common in their ecosystem helps keep the trees watered. Water in the fog collects on their needles. The water then drips to the ground and soaks down to the roots.

How do animals depend on plants?

Many animals depend on plants for food, shelter, and useful materials. Plants also give off oxygen that animals need to survive.

Food and Other Substances

Have you ever seen a caterpillar? As soon as a butterfly caterpillar hatches, it starts eating. It eats plant material constantly! Without plants, the caterpillar—and all other animals—would starve. Even animals that do not eat plants get their energy from animals that do.

Animals live in places where they can find the plants they eat. For instance, monarch butterfly caterpillars eat only milkweed plants. Many monarch butterflies spend the winter in parts of California where different kinds of milkweed are easy to find.

Monarch butterflies take in a chemical from the milkweed plants. This chemical is bitter or even poisonous to other animals. The chemical protects the monarchs from animals that might eat them. Some animals get other substances they need from the plants they eat. For example, some desert animals survive by getting water from plants.

A monarch butterfly caterpillar eats the leaf of a milkweed plant.

The praying mantis and other animals get energy from eating animals that eat plants. A branch is a perfect place for leaf insects to find food—and to hide! The insects look like the leaves they eat.

Standards Focus 4LS3.0 Living organisms depend on one another and on their environment for survival. As a basis for understanding this concept: **4LS3.c** Students know many plants depend on animals for pollination and seed dispersal, and animals depend on plants for food and shelter.

Animals such as cattle, sheep, horses, and deer depend on plants for food.

Oxygen

As you have read, plants use energy from sunlight to make their own food from water and carbon dioxide. When they make food, they also make oxygen. The plants release the oxygen into the air. This oxygen is important. People and other living things must have oxygen to get energy from the food they eat.

1. **✓Checkpoint** How do animals depend on plants for food and oxygen?

2. How do some animals use plants for protection?

Its bright colors warn predators that the monarch butterfly is not good to eat.

Monarch butterfly caterpillars eat the leaves and flowers of milkweed plants. Sometimes they even eat the seedpods.

161

Shelter and Materials

Animals depend on plants for more than just food and oxygen. Many animals find shelter among plants. You have seen pictures of insects that look like they're part of a plant. You have read that many animals in tropical rain forests live in the trees. Some spend their whole lives there! In water environments, fish and other animals hide from predators among growing plants. In the desert, large shrubs and cactus plants provide shade, hiding places, and homes for snakes, lizards, and birds.

Other animals use plants to build their own shelters. Most birds build their nests from plant materials such as twigs, moss, and leaves. Beavers build dams and homes from trees and branches.

Hummingbirds use plant fibers, moss, and lichens along with spider webs to build their tiny nests. Each nest is about the size of half of a golf ball.

162

Plants and People

People depend on plants for materials. Without trees, we would not have wood for buildings and furniture. The pages in this book were made from plant fibers. The clothes you are wearing might be made from plants, too! Many kinds of cloth are woven from plant fibers such as cotton.

Even fibers such as silk and wool that come from animals would not exist without plants. Wool is sheared from sheep that eat grasses and other plants. The silkworms that spin silk fibers live on leaves of mulberry trees. Almost everywhere you look, you will see something that came from a plant.

✓ Lesson Review

1. Give three examples of how animals depend on plants for food and three examples of how they depend on plants for shelter.

2. **Cause and Effect** How would a fire that killed many trees affect beavers living in the area?

Plant Fibers

The cotton plant provides fibers for cotton cloth.

Fibers from the flax plant can be made into yarn. Linen cloth is made from flax.

Bamboo is used for food and medicine. It is also used to build furniture.

Beavers use trees and shrubs to build their homes, called lodges. They also eat parts of the trees and other plants that grow near ponds and streams.

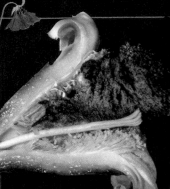

Pollen sticks to
a bat's fur.

A bee carries pollen grains
from flower to flower.

How do plants depend on animals?

Just as animals need plants, plants need animals. Many plants depend on animals to pollinate them and spread their seeds.

Bats pollinate
flowers at night.

Pollen on the Move

You read in Lesson 2 that plants must be pollinated before seeds form. Pollen is made in a flower's male parts, called stamens. The pollen has to get from the stamens to the female parts, called pistils. Some plants need help from animals to do this.

Many flowers make a sweet liquid called nectar. This is a tasty food that attracts some bats, bees, butterflies, and birds. These and other animals move from flower to flower in search of nectar. The animals are drawn by the colors of the petals and smell of the flowers. The shape of the flower directs the animal to the nectar deep inside.

As the animal eats the nectar, pollen rubs off on the animal. The pollen may then stick to the pistil of that plant or the next plant the animal visits. Bees also carry pollen back to their hives.

Standards Focus 4LS3.0 Living organisms depend on one another and on their environment for survival. As a basis for understanding this concept: **4LS3.c** Students know many plants depend on animals for pollination and seed dispersal, and animals depend on plants for food and shelter.

From Fertilization to Food

After a pollen grain lands on a pistil, a thin tube grows from the pollen down through the pistil. This pollen tube reaches egg cells inside the pistil. Sperm cells from the pollen move down the pollen tube and combine with the egg cells. This is called *fertilization*.

How does a plant make an apple, a peanut, or a pumpkin? After fertilization, the flower goes through many changes. The plant does not need the petals or stamens any longer, so they dry up and fall off. The fertilized egg develops into a fruit containing seeds. The bottom part of the pistil grows and becomes a fruit. The fruit protects the seed or seeds. Many of these fruits are good food for animals. You will see on the next page why having tasty fruit is important to a plant.

Stamen

Pollen tube

Pistil

Egg cells

Petal

1. ✅**Checkpoint** How do animals pollinate plants?

2. Why are animal pollinators attracted to some flowers but not to others?

Seeds on the Move

Some plants simply drop their seeds, and the seeds sprout. Scattering seeds, or **seed dispersal**, is not always that easy, though. Some plants can spread their seeds in the wind or through water. But many plants rely on animals to help.

Remember that many plants grow fruits around their seeds. These fruits not only protect the seeds, they also attract animals. Animals may eat the fruit but not the seeds. The seeds are often left in a place where they can sprout. A bird may pick a berry from a plant and fly some distance before eating the fruit and dropping the seed.

Other animals, such as chipmunks, mice, and squirrels, bury seeds to store and then eat later. The seeds may sprout before the animal digs them up!

Sometimes an animal swallows plant seeds with the fruit it eats. The seeds may pass through the animal's digestive system without being digested. The animal leaves the seeds with its wastes, or droppings. The seeds may be deposited and sprout into new plants far from the parent plant. The droppings provide nutrients for the plants.

The finch may carry thistle seeds away from the plant.

Seeds may sprout after chipmunks hide them in the ground.

The bird may drop the fruit in its beak far from the plant.

Wind can carry the propeller-shaped fruit and its seeds from a maple tree.

A coconut and the seed inside it can float great distances on ocean currents.

The fruit containing dandelion seeds are like tiny parachutes carried by the wind.

Seed Dispersal

Animals can carry seeds even when they do not eat them. Some seeds are inside fruits that are prickly pods called burs. These have tiny hooks that get caught on an animal's fur. The animal carries the seed away with it when it moves. When a bur finally drops to the ground, the seeds inside may grow into new plants.

Why do plants need these adaptations for seed dispersal? If all the seeds of a cherry tree fell to the ground next to the tree, many new trees might sprout. But they would have to compete with each other and with the parent tree. The parent tree's roots would absorb most of the water and nutrients from the soil. Its leaves would catch most of the sunlight. The tiny, crowded seedlings would not be able to grow. Seeds have a better chance to survive and grow well if they are scattered away from their parent plant.

Burs get tangled on an animal's fur and may be carried far from the parent plant.

✔ Lesson Review

1. Why are animals important to plants?

2. How does seed dispersal affect plant survival?

3. ✎ **Writing in Science** **Narrative** Write a story about a farmer who raises apple trees. Animals take some of the apples. In your story, explain why the animals take the apples and how this helps the apple trees.

167

Population Cycles

How do the populations of predators and their prey affect each other? Answering this question is very difficult. Many things can affect the size of a population.

Scientists use computer models to predict population changes. The models use data for just one population each of predators and prey living in a perfect habitat. The graph below shows how one model predicts the two populations will change during a month. The populations go up and down within a certain predictable range.

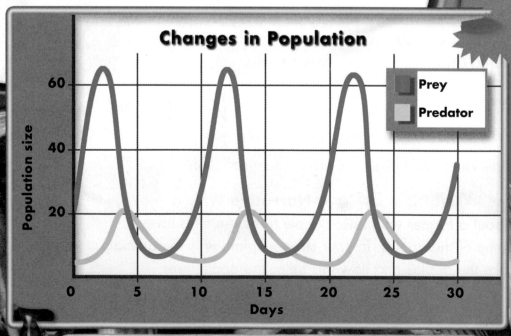

Changes in Population

Prey
Predator

Use the graph of the population cycles to answer these questions.

1. When is the population of prey the greatest?
   A. days 1, 13, and 25
   B. days 7, 14, and 21
   C. days 2, 12, and 22
   D. days 2, 5, and 8

2. What is the approximate difference between the greatest and the least number of predators?
   A. 0   B. 5   C. 15   D. 20

3. Which compares the greatest population of prey to the greatest population of predators?
   A. There are more than 3 times as many prey as predators.
   B. There are about twice as many prey as predators.
   C. There are about 10 more prey than predators.
   D. The populations are the same.

4. What happens after the predator's population becomes greater than the prey's?
   A. This never happens.
   B. The prey's population quickly decreases to zero.
   C. Both populations decrease.
   D. The prey's population immediately increases.

Lab zone Take-Home Activity

Keep a record of the amount of some type of food that is used each day in your home. Also, record the number of people who use the food each day. After one week of recording, graph your data.

Investigate How can the structure of a leaf help a plant retain water?

Materials

paper towels

water

aluminum foil

waxed paper

paper clips

What to Do

1 Wet the paper towels. Squeeze out the excess water.

2 Place one wet towel on the foil (A). Roll up the 2 remaining towels. Place 1 rolled towel on the foil as shown (B).

3 Wrap the other rolled towel in waxed paper (C). Use paper clips to keep the ends closed. Place this towel on the foil.

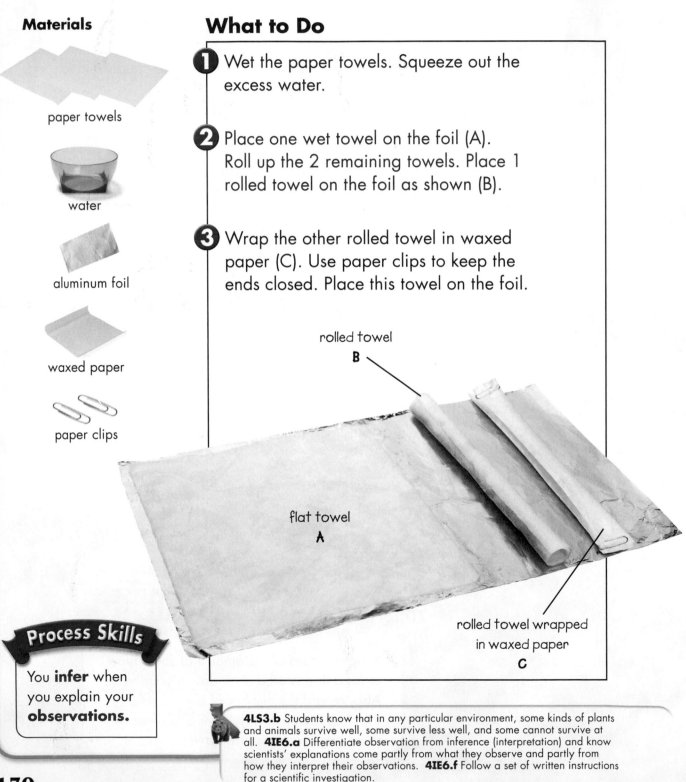

rolled towel
B

flat towel
A

rolled towel wrapped
in waxed paper
C

Process Skills

You **infer** when you explain your **observations.**

4LS3.b Students know that in any particular environment, some kinds of plants and animals survive well, some survive less well, and some cannot survive at all. **4IE6.a** Differentiate observation from inference (interpretation) and know scientists' explanations come partly from what they observe and partly from how they interpret their observations. **4IE6.f** Follow a set of written instructions for a scientific investigation.

4 After 1 day, unroll the towels.
Compare the dampness of all 3 towels.

5 Record your **observations.**

Towel	Observations
A flat towel	
B rolled towel	
C rolled towel in waxed paper	

Explain Your Results

1. Based on your **observations,** make an **inference.** How does the total area that touches the air, affect how fast a leaf loses water?

2. Compare towel B and towel C. Tell what you observed. Infer how a waxy coating may help a plant retain water.

Go Further

What might happen if you put the paper towels in a dark, sunny, or cold environment? Could it affect how fast a "leaf" loses water? Design and carry out an investigation to find out.

Chapter 5 Reviewing Key Concepts

Living things have adaptations that help them get the resources they need to survive in an ecosystem.

Lesson 1

What determines survival?
- Living things share the same limited space and resources.
- Animals have certain behaviors that help them compete.
- Sometimes living things behave in ways that help one another survive.

Lesson 2

How do environmental changes affect living things?
- Adaptations help living things compete when their environment changes.
- Plants store food to help them survive for a short time if the environment changes.
- Some animals migrate and others change their diet or color when the environment changes.

Lesson 3

How do animals depend on plants?
- Many animals use plants or plant parts for food and for a place to live.
- Plants provide places for animals to hide.
- Plants release oxygen that living things need.
- Products that people use can be made from plant parts or from animals that eat plants.

Lesson 4

How do plants depend on animals?
- Animals help pollinate plants.
- Some plant seeds are scattered by animals.

Cross-Curricular Links

English–Language Arts

Building Vocabulary

Look again at pages 146–147. Write a paragraph about the vocabulary term **competition**. Explain in your paragraph how the term is related to the picture that is behind it.

Mathematics

Decimals

A barn owl can eat one and one half times its weight in mice and other rodents each day. Write one and one half as a decimal.

Challenge!

Health

Poisonous Plants

Why do people stay healthy by eating some plants and not others? Not all plant parts are good food choices. In fact, some are poisonous to people. Use sources from the library-media center to find out about two poisonous plants. Give an oral report to share what you learned.

English–Language Arts

Pollinating Plants

Plant breeders have developed ways to pollinate plants without using animals such as bees. Find out more about how they do this. Give a presentation to your class about what you learn.

Chapter 5 Review/Test

Use Vocabulary

adaptation (p. 156)	**pollination** (p. 158)
community (p. 151)	**population** (p. 151)
competition (p. 151)	**seed dispersal** (p. 166)

Fill in the blanks with the correct vocabulary terms. If you have trouble answering a question, read the listed page again.

1. Spreading seeds to places where they can sprout is called _____.

2. _____ is the movement of pollen from stamens to pistils so seeds can form.

3. _____ takes place when two or more organisms need the same limited resources.

4. A(n) _____ is a trait that helps an organism survive.

Think About It

5. Explain the difference between an individual, a population, and a community.

6. Explain why animals claim and defend territory.

7. Why do some plants store food and water in their roots, stems, or leaves?

8. Why are fruits important to both animals and plants?

9. **Process Skills** **Predict** The data show the approximate number of bees in an apple orchard. How might the apple crop in Year 5 compare with the crop in Years 1–4? Explain your answer.

Year	1	2	3	4	5
Bees	1,200	1,100	1,400	1,150	750

10. **Draw Conclusions** Strawberry plants grow in front of your house. You notice some new strawberry plants sprouting behind your house. What could explain this?

11. **Cause and Effect** Owls and hawks eat mice. Suppose the population of hawks increases. Use a graphic organizer to show how this affects the population of owls.

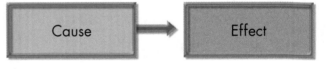

12. **Writing in Science** **Narrative** Write a report about an environment that changes in some way. Explain why some organisms survive well and others do not.

California Standards Practice

Write the letter of the correct answer.

13. Which adaptation helps whales survive in cold water?

  A seasonal diet

  B seasonal coloration

  C thick, blubbery skin

  D hibernating

14. An animal helps scatter seeds by eating which plant part?

  A fruit

  B leaves

  C roots

  D stem

15. Thin needles with a waxy coating are adaptations for what conditions?

  A cold, dry climates

  B warm, moist climates

  C rocky hillsides

  D sandy, wet soil

16. Which is the best reason to explain why some animals travel in groups?

  A They are closer to water.

  B They can find more fertile soil.

  C There is protection from predators.

  D There is less competition for grazing.

17. Plants depend on animals for

  A competition.

  B oxygen.

  C pollination.

  D population.

18. Which of the following is an example of seed dispersal?

  A pollen sticking to a bee

  B wind blowing pollen

  C apples growing on a tree

  D burs sticking to a dog's fur

19. Animals depend upon plants for

  A fertilization.

  B decomposers.

  C oxygen.

  D carbon dioxide.

20. Which part of this flower helps attract pollinating animals?

  A leaves

  B petals

  C pistil

  D stamens

Plant Biologist

Dr. Tom Dreschel is a plant biologist at NASA. He developed a way to grow plants without soil.

Plant biologists study how plants work. They study all the parts of a plant: leaves, flowers, stems, roots. They even study plant cells. They want to know how all these parts work together.

As a plant biologist, you would test plants to learn how they react to different conditions. You might test to see what happens to plants when there is no rain for months at a time. Some chemicals in the air and water can harm plants. Your tests might find out what the chemicals do to the plant. All scientists must keep detailed records of their experiments. This helps them draw conclusions and make hypotheses. They write about their work to help those who want to do similar experiments.

Some of the discoveries you make might help farmers grow bigger vegetables and fruits. You may find a way to protect plants from being eaten by insects. You might also discover a way to help plants survive long periods without water.

If working with plants sounds exciting to you, you will need to prepare. You should take math and science classes. After you graduate from high school, you will need to go to college and study plants and what they need to grow.

Lab zone Take-Home Activity

Make a list of plants that you would grow in a vegetable garden in a community plot near your home. Give reasons for your choices.

Unit B Summary

Chapter 3

How do living things interact in an ecosystem?

- Sunlight is the source of energy in most food chains and food webs.
- Plants use sunlight to make food.
- Energy and matter flow from producers to consumers to decomposers through food chains and food webs.
- Energy flows one way through an ecosystem, but matter gets recycled.

Chapter 4

How can ecosystems be described?

- The living parts of an ecosystem are its plants, animals, and other organisms.
- The nonliving parts of ecosystems include climate, air, soil, water, light, temperature, and space.
- Deserts, tropical rain forests, and coral reefs are some examples of ecosystems.

Chapter 5

How do living things survive in an ecosystem?

- Living things compete for limited resources in an ecosystem.
- Adaptations help living things survive in their environments and deal with environmental changes.
- Animals and plants depend on each other for the things they need to survive.

Experiment How does the amount of salt affect whether brine shrimp hatch?

Brine shrimp are tiny animals. They live in salt water.

Materials

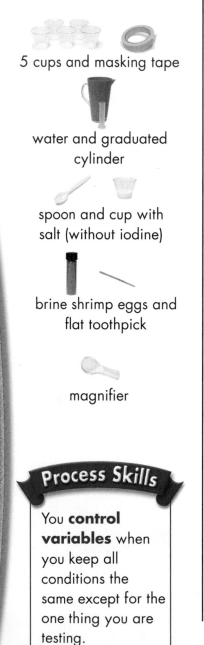

5 cups and masking tape

water and graduated cylinder

spoon and cup with salt (without iodine)

brine shrimp eggs and flat toothpick

magnifier

Process Skills

You **control variables** when you keep all conditions the same except for the one thing you are testing.

Ask a question.

Does the amount of salt in water affect how many brine shrimp eggs hatch?

State a hypothesis.

If brine shrimp eggs are put in water with no salt, a low salt level, a medium salt level, a high salt level, or a very high salt level, then in which will the most eggs hatch? Write your **hypothesis.**

Identify and control variables.

The amount of salt in the water is the **variable** you will change. Set up 4 cups of water with different amounts of salt in them, and 1 cup with no salt.

It is hard to tell if a tiny egg has hatched. It is easier to see a moving brine shrimp after it has hatched. Because of this, the variable you will observe is how many brine shrimp are moving after 4 days.

All other conditions, such as temperature, light, amount of water, and amount of brine shrimp eggs are **controlled.** They must be the same for all the cups.

4LS3.b Students know that in any particular environment, some kinds of plants and animals survive well, some survive less well, and some cannot survive at all. **4IE6.b** Measure and estimate the weight, length, or volume of objects. **4IE6.f** Follow a set of written instructions for a scientific investigation.

Test your hypothesis.

1 Use a graduated cylinder.
Put 150 mL of water in each cup.
Measure the volume carefully.

Be careful!

Wipe up spills
right away.

2 Do not add salt to Cup A. Put $\frac{1}{2}$ spoonful
of salt into Cup B. Put 1 spoonful into
Cup C. Put $1\frac{1}{2}$ spoonfuls into Cup D.
Put 3 spoonfuls into Cup E.

Label the cups A, B, C, D, and E.

3 Pick up some brine shrimp eggs on the wide end of a flat toothpick. Put them into Cup A. Put the same amount of eggs into each of the other cups.

Make a line on the toothpick to help you use the same amount each time.

4 **Observe** the cups every day. Use a magnifier. When a brine shrimp egg hatches, the shrimp starts to swim. On the chart, record how many shrimp are moving in each cup. Write none, a few, some, or many. This is a way to describe how many eggs have hatched.

In this activity your data is not numerical. You must decide what "few", "some", and "many", mean, and what each will look like. Use the same meaning each time you observe.

Collect and record your data.

Cup	How many brine shrimp are moving? (none, a few, some, or many)			
	After 1 day	After 2 days	After 3 days	After 4 days
Cup A (no salt)				
Cup B ($\frac{1}{2}$ spoonful salt)				
Cup C (1 spoonful salt)				
Cup D ($1\frac{1}{2}$ spoonfuls salt)				
Cup E (3 spoonfuls salt)				

Interpret your data.

Analyze your data. Think about the level of salt and how many brine shrimp were moving after 4 days.

State your conclusion.

What conclusion can you draw from your data?
Does it agree with your hypothesis?
Communicate your conclusion.

Go Further

How long do brine shrimp live after they hatch? Experiment further to find out. Observe the brine shrimp. Design and carry out a plan to investigate this or other questions you may have.

Show What You Know

Build a Model Ecosystem

Choose one type of ecosystem you have read about. Use a 2-L plastic bottle, clay, foam, construction paper, or other materials to build a model of your ecosystem. Include models of plants and animals that live in the ecosystem. Use research materials from the library-media center. Add labels that describe the living and nonliving parts of the ecosystem in your model. Use yarn or string to connect living things that are part of the same food web.

Seeds on the Move

Collect several different kinds of seeds. Examine each seed. Predict which ones are carried by wind, water, and animals. Then test your prediction. First, use a piece of cardboard or an electric fan to fan the seeds. Record how far each seed moved. Then, see which seeds stick to a piece of cloth or fake fur. Finally, put the seeds into a cup of water and see which ones float. Record all your observations. Based on your observations, infer how each seed travels. Identify whether your predictions were accurate.

Write a Biography

Write a "biography" of a plant you choose. Write about the plant's life and how it is affected by the living and nonliving parts of the ecosystem. Describe how the plant reacts when the environment changes. Remember that a biography is the story of a life. It should include:

- the main events of the life
- how the plant reacts to events in its life
- how the plant is part of a larger community

Read More About Life Sciences

Look for other books about Life Sciences in your library-media center. One book you may want to read is:

Nature's Green Umbrella: Tropical Rain Forests by Gail Gibbons

This book shows many plants and animals found in a tropical rain forest. You will read about the climate and conditions in this ecosystem. You will learn about rain forest plants that are used as medicine.

Full Inquiry

Using Scientific Methods

1. Ask a question.
2. State a hypothesis.
3. Identify and control variables.
4. Test your hypothesis.
5. Collect and record your data.
6. Explain your data.
7. State your conclusion.
8. Go further.

How do living things react to changes around them?

Environmental changes affect organisms.

Idea: Make a miniature pond ecosystem. Use plants and pond snails or other invertebrates. Then design an experiment to test how one environmental change will affect the living things in your model.

What plants does an insect eat?

Many living things use plants as food.

Idea: Design an experiment to see what types of plants one insect prefers to eat. Be sure to follow safety procedures in your experiment.

What environment do pill bugs prefer?

Plants and animals survive better in some environments than in others.

Idea: Design an experiment to find out which moisture or light conditions a pill bug (also called a sow bug or wood louse) prefers. Keep the pill bugs in a container that has a layer of sand and moss.

Unit B California Standards Practice

Write the letter of the correct answer.

1. **Producers make their own food. Which organisms are the main producers in almost all ecosystems?**

   A viruses

   B plants

   C plant-eating animals

   D meat-eating animals

2. **Which of the following is one reason that microorganisms are important to animals?**

   A They help with digestion.

   B They produce carbon dioxide.

   C They reduce available food.

   D They take oxygen out of the air.

3. **Which kind of plant would *most* likely be found in a low desert ecosystem?**

   A coast redwood

   B cypress tree

   C water moss

   D creosote bush

4. **The diagram shows a food web from an ecosystem.**

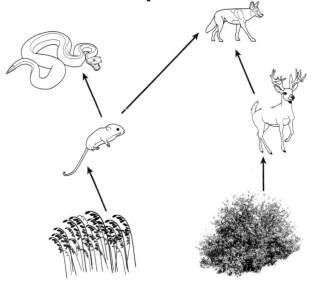

   What would *most* likely happen if the rattlesnake population increased?

   A The number of coyotes would increase.

   B The number of mice would decrease.

   C Fewer shrubs would grow.

   D Fewer grasses would grow.

5. **Which is a nonliving part of an ecosystem?**

   A plants

   B animals

   C decomposers

   D rainfall

6. The pictures show how a group of trees changed over many years.

Which of the following *most* likely explains what happened?

A Some trees competed more successfully for living space.

B Animals ate most of the trees.

C All the trees grew to full size.

D Some trees produced more seeds than others.

7. Which of the following is an adaptation that helps some plants survive in a desert ecosystem?

A tough bark that resists fire

B stems that store water

C huge, fan-shaped leaves

D leaves that fall off in the winter

8. Animals depend on plants for which of the following?

A food

B pollination

C carbon dioxide

D seed dispersal

9. Which of the following is a role of decomposers in ecosystems?

A producing food from sunlight

B producing oxygen

C returning nutrients to soil, air, and water

D making fog

10. Seeds from a plant are surrounded by a prickly bur. Which animal would *most* likely spread these seeds?

A bee

B dog

C snake

D bird

Unit B California Standards Practice

11. Which of the following is an important producer in marine ecosystems?

A algae

B baleen

C fish

D redwoods

12. The drawing shows plants in a tropical rain forest ecosystem.

Where would you expect to find *most* animals?

A in the canopy

B in the understory

C on the forest floor

D equally in all places

13. Which of the following is an adaptation that helps pitcher plants survive in poor soil?

A thick leaves that store food

B a waxy coating on its leaves

C producing sugar from water

D catching and digesting insects

14. What is the primary source of food for carnivores?

A plants

B sunlight

C other animals

D decaying matter

15. Which of the following helps bears survive in changing environments?

A a thick layer of blubber for warmth

B a diet of different kinds of food

C living and traveling in groups

D different color for each season

16. A marsh dries up over time. Which of the following would be *most* likely to happen?

  A The number of frogs would decrease.

  B The number of water plants would increase.

  C The number of migrating birds would increase.

  D The number of marsh grasses would stay the same.

17. Which of the following *best* describes a tundra ecosystem?

  A warm and dry year-round

  B hot, dry summers and cold, wet winters

  C cold and dry year-round

  D hot, humid summers and mild winters

18. Which of the following is one way decomposers help other organisms in ecosystems?

  A They produce food from sunlight.

  B They replace decaying matter with living space.

  C They spread plant seeds to other places.

  D They produce water for other organisms.

19. Which of the following is an example of a consumer?

  A fruit

  B grass

  C sparrow

  D redwood

20. The graph shows how the populations of hawks and mice in an ecosystem changed.

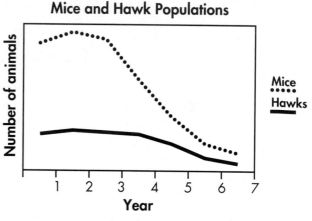

Mice and Hawk Populations

Which statement describes what probably happened?

  A A disease killed many mice, so the hawks had less food.

  B The mice suddenly moved away to escape the hawks.

  C A disease killed many hawks, so the mice had fewer predators.

  D The climate changed so the mice survived but the hawks did not.

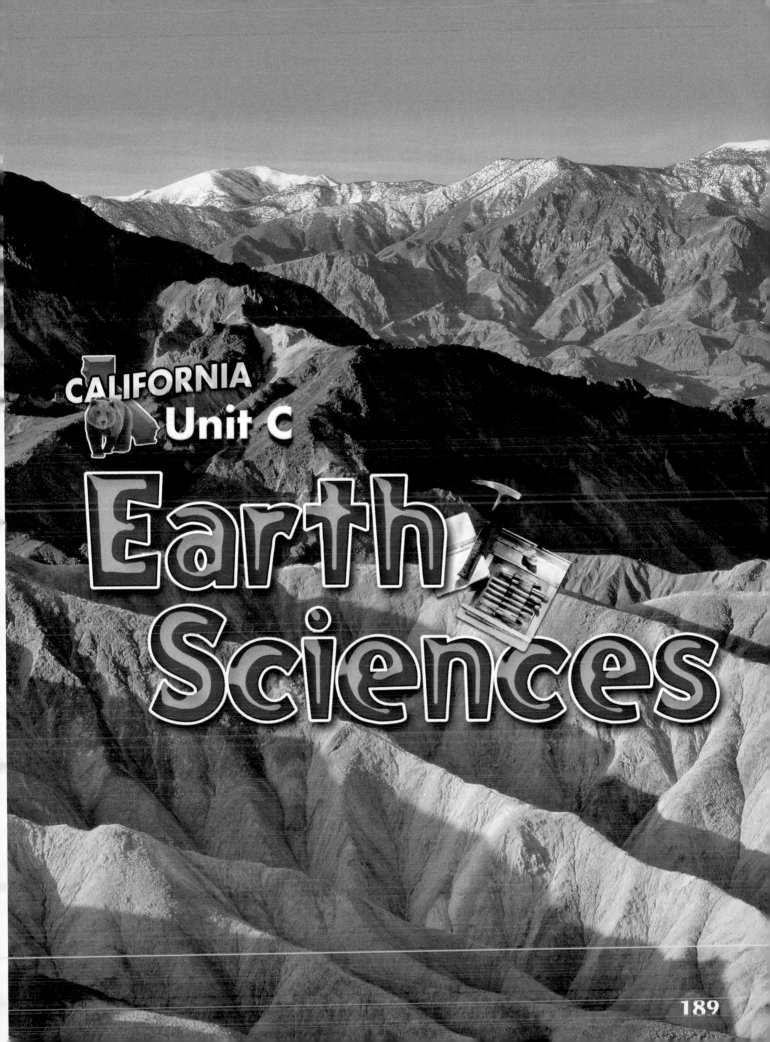

CALIFORNIA
Unit C

Earth Sciences

GOLD

Mariposa, California

Gold! The cry went out from California in the 1840s. People from all over the United States headed west to hunt for the valuable metal. Along the way, they found many other precious minerals and useful rock. Today you can see some of California's mineral riches at the California State Mining and Mineral Museum near Mariposa.

The museum has more than 13,000 minerals, rocks, gems, and fossils. You can see gold in many forms: thin sheets, narrow wires, gold nuggets, and gold crystals. You can see the largest gold nugget found during California's Gold Rush. It weighs more than 12 pounds! You can also visit a model mine that shows how Gold Rush miners worked.

Find Out More

Use resources from the library–media center to gather more information about gold and other mining in California.

- Find out where gold was found in California. Make a map showing important gold mines and when they were dug.

- Learn about the technology used in mines over time. Make a time line showing how mining has changed in California.

California
State Mining
and Mineral
Museum

- If possible, visit a mine or mine museum near you. Interview someone who works at the museum to learn more about how miners lived.

Chapter 6

Minerals and Rocks

Standards Focus Questions

- What are minerals?
- How are minerals and ores sorted?
- How are rocks classified?
- How do rocks change?

How are rocks and minerals formed?

mineral

luster

cleavage

streak

DIGITAL

Chapter 6 Vocabulary

ore

sedimentary

metamorphic

rock cycle

igneous

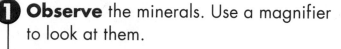
Explore How can you classify minerals?

In this activity you will come up with your own ways to classify minerals.
This will build background to help you identify these minerals.

Materials

magnifier

6 minerals

What to Do

1 **Observe** the minerals. Use a magnifier to look at them.

2 Tell how the minerals are alike and different. List words you could use to describe and sort the samples.

3 Use your ideas to **classify** your minerals into 2 to 4 groups.

Process Skills

Observing objects carefully can help you **classify** them.

Explain Your Results

How did you **classify** the minerals?

 DIGITAL Lab zone

4ES4.b Students know how to identify common rock-forming minerals (including quartz, calcite, feldspar, mica, and hornblende) and ore minerals by using a table of diagnostic properties. **4IE6.f** Follow a set of written instructions for a scientific investigation.

How to Read Science

Compare and Contrast

When you **compare** things, you tell how they are alike. When you **contrast** things, you tell how they are different. Scientists may use likenesses and differences to help them **classify**. Writers often use words or phrases to signal likenesses and differences.

- Clues such as *similar, like, all, both,* or *in the same way* show things are being compared.

- Clues such as *but, unlike,* or *however* signal differences.

Gem Guide

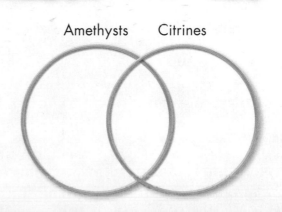

Gems are minerals that are very beautiful. Throughout history, sparkling gems named amethysts have been favorites of kings and queens. An amethyst is the purple form of the mineral quartz. Citrines are also quartz, but they are yellow or orange. Both amethysts and citrines are gemstones used in rings, necklaces, bracelets, and other jewelry. However, citrines are usually less expensive than amethysts.

Apply It!

Make a graphic organizer like the one shown. Use it to show how amethysts and citrines are alike and how they are different.

Amethysts   Citrines

You Are There!

It's summer, but you are shivering. You are deep below Earth's surface, where the temperature is a chilly 12°C (55°F). A guide is leading you through the maze of dark, damp tunnels in the California Caverns. The only sound is a constant "drip, kerplunk, gurgle." It reminds you that water formed these passageways millions of years ago. As you walk, your guide's flickering lantern shines on the cave's secrets. You see things that look like dripping icicles, blooming roses, and frozen waterfalls. How and when were these fantastic sparkling and glimmering shapes made?

Lesson 1

What are minerals?

All rocks are made of minerals. Minerals can be identified by their appearance and by testing their physical properties.

Mineral Crystals

The salt you sprinkle on your food is a mineral. The metal fork you use when you eat is made from minerals. The ceramic plate you put food on is made from minerals. **Minerals** are natural, nonliving solid crystals that make up rocks.

All over the world, each mineral has the same chemical makeup. A tiny piece of the mineral quartz from a beach in Australia has the same chemicals in it as a chunk of quartz chipped from the Sierra Nevada in California.

Scientists have identified more than 3,000 minerals. But most of the rocks in Earth's crust are made from only a very small number of them. These are often called the "rock-forming" minerals. Most rocks are made of different combinations of minerals. Each type of rock always has the same combination. Granite always contains crystals of quartz and feldspar. A few other types of rock consist of only one or two minerals. White marble is made only of the mineral calcite.

Granite, one of the most common rocks on Earth, is made of minerals.

The mineral quartz is hard and glassy.

The mineral mica forms rocks that are usually brown or black.

The mineral feldspar is often white or pink.

1. ✔ **Checkpoint** What are rock-forming minerals?

2. ✏ **Writing in Science** **Descriptive** Choose a mineral shown on this page. Write a description that a friend could use to identify which mineral you collected.

keyword: mineral code: gr4p197

197

Properties of Minerals

How can you tell one mineral from another? To identify a mineral, scientists test its properties. These include color, luster, hardness, streak, cleavage, and crystal shape. Some properties of minerals are shown on the next four pages.

Color

It's easy to see the color of a mineral. But the same mineral can be different colors. Feldspar minerals, for example, make up more than half the minerals in Earth's crust. They are often pink or white but can be other colors as well. The color of mica, another common mineral, ranges from tan to almost black. So color alone is usually not enough to identify a mineral. Scientists must look at other properties.

Pure quartz is clear. Impurities give quartz its color.

Luster

Luster is the property of how a mineral reflects light. A glassy luster is shiny, like glass. A metallic luster looks like polished metal. A soft shine can be described as a waxy, silky, or pearly luster. Some minerals may have a greasy or a dull, chalky luster.

Satin spar gypsum has a silky luster.

Galena has a metallic luster.

Sulfur is always yellow. It has a dull to glassy luster.

Talc can be white, apple green, or gray. It has a pearly luster.

Calcite has a pearly luster. It can be colorless, white, or other pale colors.

Hardness

Some minerals are harder than others. Scientists test a mineral's hardness by determining how easy it is to scratch. The Mohs scale tells how hard a mineral is by ranking it from 1 to 10. Look at the diagram of Mohs Scale. You can see that talc is the softest mineral. It has a hardness of 1. Diamond is the hardest mineral. It has a hardness of 10.

A mineral can scratch any mineral with a lower Mohs ranking. For example, the mineral quartz has a hardness of 7. Hornblende has a hardness between 5 and 6. If you rub a piece of quartz against a piece of hornblende, the quartz will scratch the hornblende.

Minerals can also be scratched by everyday items. For example, a penny has a hardness of about 3. It can scratch all minerals that have a hardness of less than 3, such as talc. A fingernail is about 2.5 on Mohs scale. It, too, scratches talc. A steel file ranks about 6.5.

Streak

You have read that you can often find different colors of the same mineral. However all colors of a certain mineral will almost always leave the same streak. **Streak** is the color of the powder that a mineral leaves when it is scratched across a special plate. Sometimes the streak is a different color than the mineral itself. For example, hematite can be silver or red. But its streak is always red.

Cinnabar has a bright red streak.

Orpiment has a pale yellow streak.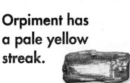

Pyrite has a green-black streak.

1. ✔Checkpoint Why is the streak test useful?

2. ✏ **Writing in Science** **Descriptive** Suppose you find a sample of a mineral. Your friend says the mineral is talc. Write a paragraph that describes how you can test some of the sample's properties to see if your friend is correct.

Mohs Scale for Hardness

10 Diamond

9 Corundum

8 Topaz

7 Quartz

6 Feldspar

5 Apatite

4 Fluorite

3 Calcite

2 Gypsum

1 Talc

Crystal Shape

The shape of a mineral is not always easy to see, but some mineral crystals have a definite shape. These crystal shapes can be helpful when trying to identify a mineral crystal.

Crystals are classified by these shapes and the angles that they form. For example, fluorite has cube-shaped crystals. Corundum crystals look more like hexagons. Scientists group crystals into six basic types or classes.

The crystals of magnetite are shaped like cubes.

A quartz crystal looks like a six-sided prism with a pyramid attached to each base.

Feldspar has crystals that are flat, with sharp edges. The edges do not form right angles.

Cleavage

Most minerals will break in definite patterns. Minerals that break along smooth, flat surfaces have **cleavage**. For example, mica has cleavage in one direction. It breaks into thin, shiny layers that are flat and smooth. Some minerals do not have any cleavage. Quartz often breaks into pieces with smooth surfaces that look like the inside of a seashell. Still other minerals splinter, like pieces of wood.

Hornblende breaks along flat, smooth surfaces that do not form right angles.

Mica breaks into thin flakes that are flat and smooth.

The mineral halite has cleavage in 3 directions. Halite is similar to table salt.

Other Properties of Minerals

In addition to the properties you have read about in this lesson, there are many other ways to identify certain minerals. Two minerals, pyrrhotite and magnetite, are attracted by a magnet. Sometimes magnetite can actually be a magnet.

Not all minerals feel the same when you touch them. Some feel sandy or gritty. Waxy minerals have a smooth, sticky feel. Earthy minerals seem powdery. Some minerals, such as opals, are smooth. Some minerals, such as gold, silver, and copper, can be shaped or cut or formed into thin wires.

Some minerals can be identified by their smell or taste. One mineral smells like garlic. Other minerals smell sour, sweet, or earthy. Halite tastes salty.

Scientists can use chemical tests to identify some minerals. For example, a drop of vinegar or another weak acid on the mineral calcite will cause gases to form. The gases escape as bubbles.

Gold is sometimes found in lumps called nuggets.

Gold

Do you know what California's state mineral is? Gold! Gold is a rare mineral, which makes it valuable. For centuries, people have used gold to make jewelry or to trade as money. It has a shiny, metallic luster. It is yellow, and its streak is golden yellow. Gold is a soft metal, so it can be pounded into shapes or thin sheets.

Sometimes people have found large amounts of gold in one place. Others flock to that place. They hope to find gold and become rich. In January 1848, gold was discovered at Sutter's Mill near Coloma in northern California. The discovery started the greatest gold rush in the United States.

The magnetite in this lodestone attracts objects that contain iron.

Vinegar fizzes on limestone that is made of calcite. The fizzing is caused by the acid in the vinegar reacting with the calcite. The reaction gives off carbon dioxide.

✓ Lesson Review

1. What are some of the properties used to identify minerals?

2. **Writing in Science** **Summarize** Write a summary of this lesson that identifies its main idea and supporting details.

Lesson 2

How are minerals and ores sorted?

Many resources are found below Earth's surface. Ores contain important metals or other substances that people use.

Resources in Rocks

Rocks contain many valuable resources. An **ore** is a rock rich in valuable minerals that can be removed from Earth's crust. People mine ore to get the minerals from it. These minerals might contain metals such as zinc or copper. In general, ore deposits are not common everywhere in Earth's crust. People use many different methods to find them.

People use mineral resources in various ways. For example, iron ore contains a lot of the metal iron. Miners remove iron ore from the ground. Then the ore is crushed and heated. The iron is separated out. Often the iron is mixed with other materials to make steel. Steel is used to make tools and machines. Cars, skyscrapers, and even paper clips are made of steel.

Other mineral resources include gypsum and mica. Gypsum is a white mineral. It is used in plaster and paint. Mica is also used in paint. Halite, or rock salt, and sylvite, which is used to make fertilizer, are other useful minerals.

How Ores Are Mined

Ores are often many meters below Earth's surface. In order to get to the ores, people have to get through huge amounts of soil and rock. First, workers dig an open pit. Then they build vertical mine shafts. The shafts reach all the way down to the ore. Miners enter the shaft through openings built along it. They use machines to dig out the ore. Elevators carry it out of the mine.

Standards Focus 4ES4.b Students know how to identify common rock-forming minerals (including quartz, calcite, feldspar, mica, and hornblende) and ore minerals by using a table of diagnostic properties.

The iron from hematite may be used in many products made of steel.

Hematite

Look at the picture in the corner of a lumpy gray mineral. This mineral is called hematite. Much of the iron people use comes from this mineral. Hematite is made of iron and oxygen. About seven-tenths of hematite is pure iron. Hematite has different forms. It can have shiny six-sided crystals or coarse grains. The crystals are often gray, and the coarse-grained ores are reddish-brown. Red-colored hematite, such as the ore you see at the left, can be used to make red paint. It is also purified and used to polish glass.

People have found hematite in many places. In California it has been found in rocks near silver mines and in quarries. If you ever see red soil, you may be looking at hematite!

The iron for this skillet came from iron ores such as hematite.

This park bench from the early 1900s was made of iron.

1. **Checkpoint** What is hematite? What are its properties?

2. **Writing in Science** **Narrative** Write a paragraph that tells how ores are used.

Galena

The metal lead is found in a mineral ore called galena. Galena is gray and has a metallic luster. It is the most common mineral that contains lead, and it is easy to mine. People have used galena for about 5,000 years!

In California, two important sources of galena are near Darwin in Inyo County and the Jamestown mine in Tuolumne County.

Galena has a metallic luster. You can see its crystals in this picture.

Lead

Have you ever had an X ray of your teeth? You might have worn a special, heavy apron to protect the rest of your body from the rays. This apron was probably lined with lead from galena. Lead can block harmful radiation. It is also a poor conductor of electricity.

Lead is a dense, blue-gray metal. It seems heavy compared to the same size sample of other metals. Lead is easy to shape. It is used in building materials. It can be used to join pieces of colored glass in stained-glass windows. In the past, it was used to color paints and pottery and to make pipes that brought drinking water to buildings. It was also added to the materials used to make glassware for foods. But long-term exposure to lead is poisonous to people. Paints, pipes and glassware are usually made from other materials today.

Lead inside aprons protects people while X-ray pictures are taken.

Copper

Copper was one of the first metals used by people thousands of years ago. It is a shiny metal that is easy to shape and to make into wire and pipes.

Copper is found in many forms. Often it is found as the pure metal in rocks formed from lava. (You will read more about this kind of rock in the next lesson.) People crush the rock and separate the copper. Copper is also found in other minerals and ores. Some of these ores are bright blue or green! One important copper ore is called chalcocite.

Copper pipes are often used to carry water.

Heat flows easily through copper. It is popular for cooking pots.

Electricity flows easily through copper. This makes it a good choice for electrical wires. Heat, too, flows easily through copper products such as pots and pans. Copper is also used to make motors and generators. It can be mixed with other metals to form bronze and brass.

Copper is found in many places. During the 1800s, people in California mined copper in Del Norte County in the north, around Placerville in El Dorado County near the Nevada border, and near Clark Mountain in the Mojave Desert—and in many places in between! Today, the largest copper mine is near Salt Lake City, Utah.

The Statue of Liberty is covered with copper sheets. Copper turns green when it is exposed to moist air.

1. ✔**Checkpoint** From what ore is lead produced?

2. **Compare and Contrast** Choose two of the ores you have read about. Use a graphic organizer to compare and contrast the ores you choose.

TARGET SKILL

Using Properties to Identify Minerals

You read in Lesson 1 about some of the properties scientists use to identify minerals. Scientists observe all the properties of a mineral. Then, they compare their observations to a table. The table shows the properties of many known minerals. It can take a lot of practice and training to identify the minerals correctly.

The table below has some of the properties of ten minerals and ores. Use it to identify the samples on the next page.

Mineral	Color	Luster	Hardness	Streak	Other
Mica	dark brown, black, silver white	pearly	2–2.5	white	flakes when peeled
Feldspar	colorless or many colors, including beige, pink, grey, bluish-green	glassy or pearly	6–6.5	white	group of Earth's most common minerals
Calcite	one color, ranging from colorless to white, pink, yellow, greenish, red	ranges from glassy to dull	3	white	fizzes when vinegar is poured on it
Quartz	clear (may be colored by impurities)	glassy	7	white	fractures along curved surfaces, like broken glass
Magnetite	black	shiny, metallic	5.5–6	black	magnetic
Pyrite	gold	metallic	6–6.5	greenish-black	called "fool's gold" because it looks like gold
Hornblende	dark-green to black	silky	5–6	pale gray to gray	often has long, dark crystals; cleavage in 2 directions
Hematite	silver-gray or red	metallic or nonmetallic	5–6	reddish brown	feels grainy
Galena	lead-gray	metallic	2.5	gray	heavy for its size
Copper	copper red	metallic	2.5–3	copper red	tarnishes black, blue, or green

This mineral is smooth and has a glassy luster. Its hardness is 7.

This mineral has a metallic luster. Its hardness is 6 to 6.5, and its streak is greenish-black.

This smooth mineral has a glassy luster and a white streak. It is rated 3 on Mohs scale.

This mineral is black and has a shiny luster. It is one of the few magnetic minerals.

This mineral has a hardness of 5 or 6. It can have a pale gray to gray streak even though it is dark-green to black in color.

This mineral's luster is glassy or pearly. Its streak is white.

This mineral can be peeled into thin sheets. It is soft and smooth with a hardness of 2 to 2.5.

This mineral ore has a metallic luster and reddish streak. Over time, its color can change to black, blue, or green.

This mineral ore has a reddish-brown streak. It may be either metallic or nonmetallic. It has a hardness of 5 to 6.

This mineral ore feels heavy. Its streak and color are gray. It has a metallic luster.

✓ **Lesson Review**

1. Name three common ores or ore minerals.

2. ✎ **Writing in Science** **Descriptive** Choose a mineral or ore that interests you. Use materials from the library-media center to learn its properties. Write a description of the mineral or ore that includes its important properties and where it is found.

Obsidian looks like glass. It forms when lava cools very rapidly after the eruption of a volcano.

Pumice forms from lava that has lots of trapped gas bubbles. Some pumice has so many tiny pockets of air that it floats!

Basalt is a quickly cooled igneous rock. Most of Earth's crust beneath the oceans is basalt.

Lesson 3

How are rocks classified?

Rocks constantly change form both above and below Earth's surface. These changes produce three main kinds of rocks.

Igneous Rocks

Scientists classify rocks. One important way they do this is based on how rocks form. Some rocks form from other rocks that have melted! Rock below Earth's surface can be so hot that it is partially melted. This molten rock is called magma. **Igneous** rocks form from this molten rock. In fact, the word *igneous* comes from a Latin word that means "fire." Igneous rocks may form above or below Earth's surface. Usually these rocks are hard. They don't have layers, but they often have crystals that interlock.

If you have seen pictures of a volcano erupting, you have seen magma exploding onto Earth's surface. After it reaches the surface, the molten rock is called lava. Sometimes lava oozes from a volcano like a red-hot river. Sometimes, it is hurled out of a volcano in hot, gooey globs.

Lava Cooling Quickly

Once it's on Earth's surface, the lava cools quickly. It may harden into solid igneous rock in just a few days. As the lava cools, mineral crystals form. However, when lava cools quickly, there is not much time for the crystals to form. Any crystals that do form are very small. Pumice is an igneous rock that forms when air cools lava quickly. Water can also cool the lava. Basalt is a dark green or black rock that often forms under the ocean. The ocean water quickly cools the lava. Many islands are made of basalt.

Standards Focus 4ES4.0 The properties of rocks and minerals reflect the processes that formed them. As a basis for understanding this concept:
4ES4.a Students know how to differentiate among igneous, sedimentary, and metamorphic rocks by referring to their properties and methods of formation (rock cycle).

Granite is slowly cooled igneous rock. Its large crystals of quartz, feldspar, and mica are easy to see.

Pegmatite contains the same minerals as granite. It cools and hardens very slowly. It often has very large crystals.

Gabbro cools slowly. The minerals in it may separate into layers.

The Devils Postpile formed about 100,000 years ago.

Devils Postpile National Monument

Along the San Joaquin River in the Sierra Nevada is a national monument called the Devils Postpile. It is made mostly of basalt, which formed from a flow of lava. As the rock cooled, cracks formed in it, making the long, post-like columns. Until ten or twelve thousand years ago, glaciers were found in the area. The moving ice wore away one side of the postpile. The wall of columns left by the glacier is more than 18 meters tall

Magma Cooling Slowly

Some igneous rocks form more slowly beneath Earth's surface. Magma rises slowly toward the surface. As it rises, it might force open cracks to make space. In some cases, the magma might melt some of the surrounding rock. The magma then slowly cools. Crystals of minerals form in the rock. Because the magma cools slowly, the crystals have time to grow large. Over time, the magma cools and hardens into igneous rock. The process below Earth's surface can take more than a million years!

Granite is one common slowly cooled rock. Granite has large crystals of quartz, feldspar, and mica. It forms when magma cools slowly underground. Pegmatite and gabbro are two other rocks that form from magma that cools slowly.

Igneous rocks have many uses. Granite is very hard. This makes it a good choice for buildings such as offices, libraries, and schools. It is also used for tabletops and other things inside buildings. The concrete that you see in sidewalks might even contain pieces of igneous rocks!

1. ✓**Checkpoint** What are igneous rocks?
2. Does gabbro usually have large or small crystals? Explain how you know.

Sedimentary Rocks

Look at the sandstone cliffs shown at the bottom of this page. What do you notice? The cliffs may look like a stack of pancakes or sheets of paper. These layers show that the cliff is made of sedimentary rock. **Sedimentary** rocks form when layers of sediments settle on top of one another and harden. Sediments are made up of soil, shells, bits of rock, and the remains of dead plant and animal matter.

Water, wind, ice, and gravity move sediments from one place to another. Over time, sediments settle in layers on land or on the bottom of oceans, rivers, and lakes. Some particles of sediment are smooth and round. Others have sharp corners.

Layering

Newer layers press the older layers together. The weight of the layers and sticky clay minerals in the sediment hold the particles together. Natural chemicals may also help cement them. Each layer of sediment settles on top of older layers. So the newest layer is usually on top.

Layers of rock at Earth's surface are usually younger than the layers below them. This fact helps scientists who study the ages of rocks as well as those who study things that have lived on Earth. Fossils in a lower layer are probably older than fossils in a higher layer.

The layers of sedimentary rock are easy to see in these cliffs.

DIGITAL

Look for Active Art animations at www.pearsonsuccessnet.com

Blocks of limestone are fixed to a building frame. Solid blocks of limestone are very heavy. They are rarely used in tall buildings.

Types and Uses of Sedimentary Rock

How can you tell if a rock is sedimentary? Rocks with layers that you can see are likely to be sedimentary rocks. Often, broken grains from older rocks are cemented together in layers of sedimentary rock.

Scientists classify sedimentary rocks according to the materials in the sediment. One type of sedimentary rock forms from materials that were once living things. Limestone, for example, is made of hard skeletons and shells of sea animals that lived long ago. The remains settled in layers. Dissolved minerals hold the sediments together. Limestone is useful for making cement, glass, and many other products.

Sandstone is another type of sedimentary rock. It is made of pieces of mineral or rock that are each about the size of a grain of sand. Sandstone is often used for buildings and decorative objects such as statues. In many cities in the eastern United States, homes called brownstones were built from a reddish-brown type of sandstone.

A third kind of sedimentary rock is made of very tiny particles. These particles usually settle at the bottom of lakes or oceans. Shale and mudstone are two examples of this kind of rock. Like limestone, shale is used to make cement.

Limestone can form from tiny bits of skeletons and shells.

Sandstone can form from quartz sand.

Mudstone forms from very tiny particles.

1. ✓**Checkpoint** What is sedimentary rock?

TARGET SKILL

2. **Compare and Contrast** Describe how limestone and sandstone are alike and how they are different.

211

Metamorphic Rock

The temperature is high deep inside Earth. The rock there is also under a lot of pressure. The weight of the rocks above squeezes and presses on it. The heat and pressure can change how the particles in the rock are arranged. This process changes the properties of the rock. It can even form new minerals. When this happens, **metamorphic** rock forms. The word *metamorphic* means "change of form." Metamorphic rocks can form from sedimentary rocks, igneous rocks, and even other metamorphic rocks.

As metamorphic rocks form, they can change in several ways. Heat and pressure may cause the mineral crystals in the rock to change. The new crystals might be a different shape or size. Sometimes the chemicals in the rock form new types of minerals.

Metamorphic rocks are usually hard. Sometimes the heat and pressure cause the rock particles to form layers. This causes some metamorphic rocks to chip into flat sheets and slabs. Look at the pictures at the top of the next page. You can see the fine, thin layers in slate that form under lower pressure. You can see the rougher layers in gneiss that form when the pressure is very high.

The metamorphic rocks marble, schist, and gneiss in the Sierra Nevada of California were once limestone and sandstone.

Phyllite forms from sedimentary rock. Layering of the minerals mica and chlorite makes it shiny.

Slate forms from the sedimentary rock shale. Slate easily splits into layers.

Gneiss can form from sedimentary or igneous rock. It forms at very high pressures and temperatures.

Uses of Metamorphic Rock

You can see examples of metamorphic rock in many buildings around you. In the past, slate was often used in roofs because it is a strong material. It was used in classrooms for chalkboards. Slate is also used in patios and walkways. Marble has been used in buildings and sculptures since ancient times. It is a useful rock for carving because it does not break easily. Floor tiles, stone walls, and some of the gravel you see in walkways and driveways often come from metamorphic rocks.

✓ Lesson Review

1. What causes sedimentary or igneous rock to turn into metamorphic rock?

2. **Writing in Science** **Descriptive** Choose one igneous rock, one sedimentary rock, and one metamorphic rock. Describe how the rocks you choose are similar and different.

Lesson 4

How do rocks change?

Rocks are always changing from one form into another in a process called the rock cycle. Heat, pressure, chemical reactions, and other forces drive this cycle.

The Rock Cycle

Rocks are constantly being formed and destroyed. The recycling of old rock into new is an ongoing process called the **rock cycle**. Unlike the life cycle of a plant or animal, it is not a one-way flow of events. Rocks can change from one kind to another in any order. Or they can stay the same for millions of years. You can see examples of how rock can change by following the arrows.

Granite

Granite is an igneous rock that has large grains. It forms when magma cools slowly. Under high heat and pressure deep inside Earth, granite's particles change. It becomes a metamorphic rock called gneiss.

Gneiss

The minerals in gneiss are arranged in alternating patterns. Over time, rain can wear down any gneiss that is on Earth's surface. The rain and wind carry away tiny particles of the rock. The particles form layers. The layers harden into sedimentary rock. Shale is one type of sedimentary rock that forms from thin layers of tiny particles.

Standards Focus 4ES4.0 The properties of rocks and minerals reflect the processes that formed them. As a basis for understanding this concept:
4ES4.a Students know how to differentiate among igneous, sedimentary, and metamorphic rocks by referring to their properties and methods of formation (rock cycle).

Shale

Tiny clay sediments settle on the bottom of oceans and lakes, forming shale. Shale is a soft sedimentary rock that often contains fossils. Shale that is exposed to heat and pressure can turn into much harder rock called slate. Slate does not usually have fossils because the heat and pressure destroy them. The minerals in slate are arranged so that it splits easily into layers.

Slate

Slate is a metamorphic rock. Heat and pressure can change slate into other metamorphic rocks, such as a rock called phyllite.

Phyllite

Phyllite can change again into yet another kind of metamorphic rock! It can become a metamorphic rock called schist. Schist has larger grains than phyllite or shale.

Schist

You might expect the cycle to end here, but it does not. Deep within Earth, schist and other rocks get hot enough to melt. The melted schist cools and becomes new igneous rock—perhaps granite!

1. **✓Checkpoint** Summarize how granite can change into schist and back into granite.

2. ✎ **Writing in Science**
   Narrative Write a story from the point of view of a particle of granite. Describe what happens to the particle as it moves through the rock cycle.

How Rock Can Change

Look at the diagram on these two pages. As you can see, all three types of rock can change from one type to another at some point in the cycle. Not all rocks complete the entire cycle. For example, rocks deep in Earth's crust may never get to the surface. Sedimentary rock may melt and become igneous rock without ever becoming metamorphic rock.

Magma explodes onto Earth's surface.

Lava cools quickly to form igneous rock.

Magma cools slowly beneath Earth's surface and hardens into igneous rock.

Igneous rock under heat and pressure becomes metamorphic rock.

Heat melts metamorphic rock or sedimentary rock into magma deep within Earth.

Ash from volcanoes forms layers of sediment.

Layers of sediment harden into rock.

Some sedimentary rock wears away to form new layers of sediment.

Igneous and metamorphic rocks wear over time and form layers of sediment.

Heat and pressure change sedimentary rock into metamorphic rock.

✔ **Lesson Review**

1. Explain how igneous, sedimentary, and metamorphic rocks form.

2. ✎ **Writing** in **Science**

   Descriptive Choose one type of rock. Write a paragraph that describes to a younger student how the rock can change as it passes through the rock cycle.

Classifying Solid Figures

Mineral crystals often have the shapes of familiar solid figures. Sometimes a crystal is a combination of two or more familiar shapes. This table shows how some solid figures are classified.

Prisms

A prism has two congruent, parallel bases. Its faces are parallelograms. A prism is named by the shape of its bases.

Pyramids

The base of a pyramid is a polygon. The faces are triangles that meet at a point. A pyramid is named by the shape of its base.

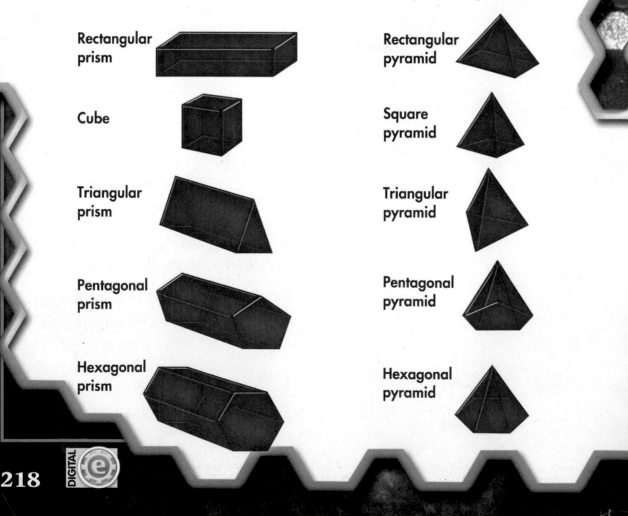

Prisms	Pyramids
Rectangular prism	Rectangular pyramid
Cube	Square pyramid
Triangular prism	Triangular pyramid
Pentagonal prism	Pentagonal pyramid
Hexagonal prism	Hexagonal pyramid

This crystal is shaped like a cube.

This crystal has two pyramids and a prism.

Part of this crystal is a pyramid. The other part is a hexagonal prism.

Write which solid shape or shapes you see in each picture.

1.

2.

3.

4. If a mineral crystal were shaped like a cube with a pyramid at each end, what kind of pyramid would be at each end? Explain your answer.

Lab zone Take-Home Activity

Look for small rocks that are shaped like solid figures. Collect samples, and glue them to cardboard or posterboard. Beneath each rock, write a description of the solid shape or shapes that you see.

Lab zone Guided Inquiry

Investigate How can you identify minerals?

You can identify common rock-forming minerals using a table of their properties.

Materials

6 minerals

magnifier

streak plate

What to Do

1 Use a magnifier to **observe** the minerals.

2 Record their color and luster in your Table of Observed Properties (p. 221).

3 Rub each one on a streak plate. Record the color of its streak.

Be careful!

Put the streak plate flat on the table.

D

Table of Diagnostic Properties

Mineral	Properties			
	Color	Luster (glassy or metallic)	Streak	Hardness
Rose quartz	pink	glassy	white	7
Calcite	white/clear	glassy	white	3
Feldspar	varied	glassy	white	6
Mica (muscovite)	varied	glassy	white	2.5
Hornblende	dark green to black	glassy	pale gray to gray	5.5
Pyrite	gold	metallic	green to brown to black	6.5

Process Skills

You **classify** objects when you sort them according to properties you **observe.**

220 DIGITAL Lab zone

4ES4.b Students know how to identify common rock-forming minerals (including quartz, calcite, feldspar, mica, and hornblende) and ore minerals by using a table of diagnostic properties. **4IE6.f** Follow a set of written instructions for a scientific investigation.

4 The hardness scale goes from 1 to 10. The softest is 1. The hardest is 10.

5 Scratch mineral A against mineral F. Compare the properties you observed with the Table of Diagnostic Properties (p. 220). Identify each mineral.

Is mineral A harder than mineral F? Does your result agree with the numbers in your Table of Observed Properties?

Table of Observed Properties

Mineral	Observed Properties				Identity of Mineral
	Color	Luster (glassy or metallic)	Streak	Hardness	
Mineral A				6	
Mineral B				not measured	
Mineral C				not measured	
Mineral D				not measured	
Mineral E				not measured	
Mineral F				2.5	

Explain Your Results

1. What is mineral E? Which of its properties did you **observe?**

2. What properties did you use to describe and identify the minerals?

Go Further

How could you classify or sort your minerals based on their observed properties? Share your idea and try it out.

Focus on the BIG Idea

Minerals are formed by natural processes. Rocks are made from different combinations of minerals.

Lesson 1

What are minerals?

- A mineral is a natural, nonliving crystal solid found in Earth.
- Rocks are made of combinations of minerals.
- Scientists identify minerals according to properties such as hardness, luster, streak, color, and cleavage.

Lesson 2

How are minerals and ores sorted?

- An ore is a rock containing a valuable substance that can be mined from Earth.
- Mineral ores are used to make useful products such as steel.
- Scientists sort and classify minerals according to properties.

Lesson 3

How are rocks classified?

- Igneous rock forms when molten magma or lava cools and hardens.
- Sedimentary rock forms when sediments are deposited and then harden into rock.
- Metamorphic rocks form when any type of rock is exposed to heat and pressure.

Lesson 4

How do rocks change?

- Rocks are constantly undergoing changes in a process called the rock cycle.
- Over time, all rocks can change into any of the three types of rocks.

Cross-Curricular Links

English–Language Arts

Building Vocabulary

Look again at page 193. Look at the pictures of the rocks behind the terms **igneous, sedimentary,** and **metamorphic.** Write a paragraph explaining how these terms relate to the pictures and to the term **rock cycle.**

Mathematics

Distance and Time

When the Hawaiian volcano Mauna Loa erupted in 1950, the lava flowed a distance of about 27 kilometers to the ocean. After 3 hours, the lava reached the ocean. About how fast did the lava flow?

Visual and Performing Arts

Draw a Mineral

A green mineral has a glassy luster. It has a hardness of 4 and a white streak. Draw what this mineral might look like. Also draw what happens when you try to scratch it with a penny or another object that ranks lower on Mohs scale.

Challenge!

English–Language Arts

Moon Rocks

Astronauts have brought samples of rocks from the Moon back to Earth. How do Moon rocks differ from Earth rocks? How are they similar? What are their properties? Use research materials to find out. Then write an expository composition describing what you learn.

Use Vocabulary

cleavage (p. 200)	**ore** (p. 202)
igneous (p. 208)	**rock cycle** (p. 214)
luster (p. 198)	**sedimentary** (p. 212)
metamorphic (p. 212)	**streak** (p. 199)
mineral (p.197)	

Fill in the blanks with the correct vocabulary terms. If you have trouble answering a question, read the listed page again.

1. A natural material that makes up rock is a(n) _____.

2. The _____ of a mineral sample is the color of the powder the mineral leaves when is scratched on a special plate.

3. Weathered rock, soil, and the remains of dead plant and animal matter that become cemented together over time make up the layers of _____ rock.

4. Heat and pressure may change one type of rock into _____ rock.

5. The way a mineral reflects light is called _____.

6. Cooled lava becomes _____ rock.

7. _____ is mineral-rich rock that can be removed from Earth's crust.

Think About It

8. The oldest layers of sedimentary rock are usually the deepest layers. Why?

9. Explain how metamorphic rock can change into igneous rock.

10. **Process Skills** **Infer** Why are fossils not found in igneous rock?

11. **Classify** A steel file ranks 6.5 on Mohs scale. Which minerals listed in the table would it scratch?

Mineral	Mohs Rating
Augite	5.5
Cinnabar	2.5
Emerald	7.5
Magnetite	6
Sapphire	9

12. **TARGET SKILL** **Compare and Contrast** Use a graphic organizer and the table on page 206 to compare and contrast the rock-forming minerals feldspar and quartz.

Feldspar   Quartz

13. **Writing in Science**
Descriptive You are hiking and find some interesting sedimentary rocks. Write a description of the rocks with details about the colors, textures, and other things you might observe.

California Standards Practice

Write the letter of the correct answer.

14. Which of the following is a physical property used to identify minerals?

A color

B reaction with vinegar

C age

D temperature

15. Every type of rock is

A formed the same way.

B soil mixed with sediment.

C made of one or more minerals.

D sediments from plants.

16. Which statement describes an igneous rock formed by magma slowly cooling below Earth's surface?

A It has very tiny crystals.

B It has large crystals.

C It does not have crystals.

D Its crystals settle in layers.

17. Which term describes old rock naturally breaking down and forming new rock?

A metamorphosis

B the rock cycle

C mining

D erosion

18. Which of the following minerals is an ore for lead?

A hematite

B galena

C copper

D magnetite

19. What property of minerals does Mohs scale measure?

A cleavage

B luster

C streak

D hardness

20. Which is the best title for the drawing below?

A Igneous Rock

B Metamorphic Rock

C Sedimentary Rock

D The Rock Cycle

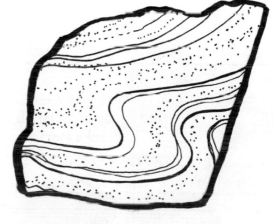

Doug Ming

Dr. Douglas Ming is a NASA scientist who studies soils. He is a member of the Mars Exploration Rover team at the Johnson Space Center in Houston, Texas.

Dr. Douglas Ming is a NASA soil scientist. For 15 years Dr. Ming and his team studied ways that different watering methods affect plant systems. One of the team's goals was to grow plants in conditions like those on the Moon or Mars. As part of his research, Dr. Ming lived in an enclosed environment for a month. He was able to see what it would be like to live, work, and conduct experiments on Mars. At the same time, the NASA rover *Sojourner* was on Mars testing technologies that led to the robot rovers *Spirit* and *Opportunity*.

Even before *Spirit* and *Opportunity* landed on Mars in 2004, NASA scientists were working on ways to protect explorers from the harsh Martian atmosphere and radiation levels. The rovers sent new data that help Dr. Ming and others identify materials in the Martian soil that future explorers can use. The rovers also measure chemicals in the dust that might harm equipment.

Another instrument is looking for evidence of water in the soil and rocks of Mars. The mineral hematite is one of the rocks that *Spirit* has examined. On Earth, hematite is sometimes linked to a watery environment. Measurements from this rock will help scientists learn about the link between water, hematite, and past environments on Mars. These data also show that weathering occurs on Mars.

The work of Dr. Ming and his team will be used in planning spacesuits, habitats, and vehicles for the first human visitors on Mars.

Hematite and other materials make Mars appear red.

Lab zone Take-Home Activity

Use sources from the library-media center to find more information about hematite. Write a paragraph that summarizes what you learn.

Chapter 7

Our Changing Earth

CALIFORNIA Standards Preview

4ES5.0 Waves, wind, water, and ice shape and reshape Earth's land surface. As a basis for understanding this concept:

4ES5.a Students know some changes in earth are due to slow processes, such as erosion, and some changes are due to rapid processes, such as landslides, volcanic eruptions, and earthquakes.

4ES5.b Students know natural processes, including freezing and thawing and the growth of roots, cause rocks to break down into smaller pieces.

4ES5.c Students know moving water erodes landforms, reshaping the land by taking it away from some places and depositing it as pebbles, sand, silt, and mud in other places (weathering, transport, and deposition).

4IE6.0 Scientific progress is made by asking meaningful questions and conducting careful investigations. As a basis for understanding this concept and addressing the content of the other three strands, students should develop their own questions and perform their own investigations. (Also **4IE6.b**, **4IE6.c**, **4IE6.d**, **4IE6.f**)

Standards Focus Questions

- How does Earth's surface slowly change?

- What causes physical weathering?

- How does weathered material move?

- What causes rapid changes to landforms?

How is Earth's surface shaped and reshaped?

landform

fault

earthquake

volcano

228

DIGITAL

Chapter 7 Vocabulary

weathering

erosion

deposition

landslide

soil

transport

Explore How can you model the wearing away of a mineral?

Model the wearing away of a mineral. The chalk represents the mineral. The wearing away is caused by the action of the rocks and water.

Materials

plastic jar with lid

balance with gram cubes

4 pieces of chalk and 8 rocks

timer or clock with second hand

water and graduated cylinder

spoon and paper towel

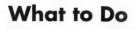

Process Skills

You can **measure** mass in grams and volume in milliliters.

What to Do

1 Pour 250 mL of water into a jar. Add chalk. After 1 minute remove the chalk with the spoon and dry with the paper towel. **Measure** the total mass of the chalk.

2 Put the chalk and rocks in the jar. Cover tightly. Shake for 4 minutes.

water (250 mL)
8 rocks
4 pieces of chalk

3 Remove the chalk and dry. **Estimate** and then measure the total mass of the chalk.

Explain Your Results

1. **Communicate** How did the pieces of chalk appear after you shook them?

2. Compare your **measurements.** How did the mass of the chalk change?

4ES5.0 Waves, wind, water, and ice shape and reshape Earth's land surface.
4ES5.b Students know natural processes, including freezing and thawing and the growth of roots, cause rocks to break down into smaller pieces. **4IE6.b** Measure and estimate the weight, length, or volume of objects. (Also **4IE6.f**)

How to Read Science

Reading Skills

Sequence

A **sequence** is a series of actions that take place in a certain order.

- A writer might use clue words such as *first, then, next,* and *finally* to **communicate** a sequence.
- An artist might use numbers and labels in a drawing to show a sequence.

Science Article

Volcano

How does a volcano erupt? First, pressure and heat melt rock inside Earth. This material is magma, a hot, thick liquid mixed with gases. Then, some of the magma rises through cracks in the rock above it. Next, the liquid rock and gases build up pressure on the rock at the surface. Finally, the pressure becomes so great that it pushes the melted rock, gases, and pieces of rock onto Earth's surface.

Apply It!

Make a sequence of how a volcano forms. Use the information you read to complete a graphic organizer like this one.

You Are There!

As you hike in the mountains, you reach the top of a tall peak. Not far away, a mountain goat stands on a ledge that juts out over the valley. What a view! You see the valley far below. Beyond the valley is a mountain that's even taller than the one you just climbed. The mountain has very steep sides. You begin to wonder—why is that mountain higher than the one you're on? Why are its sides so steep? Where did that ledge come from?

Standards Focus 4ES5.0 Waves, wind, water, and ice shape and reshape Earth's land surface. As a basis for understanding this concept:
4ES5.a Students know some changes in earth are due to slow processes, such as erosion, and some changes are due to rapid processes, such as landslides, volcanic eruptions, and earthquakes.
4ES5.c Students know moving water erodes landforms, reshaping the land by taking it away from some places and depositing it as pebbles, sand, silt, and mud in other places (weathering, transport, and deposition).

DIGITAL

How does Earth's surface slowly change?

Earth's surface is constantly changing. It is worn away by many things. These include water, ice, temperature changes, chemicals, and living things. Sometimes these forces work quickly, and sometimes they take a long time.

Earth's Crust

The outer surface of Earth is a layer of rock called the crust. The crust covers all of Earth. In places such as the oceans, the crust is under water. It is mostly basalt. Under the continents, Earth's crust is mostly granite.

A mountain is one of many shapes that Earth's crust can have. Earth's surface also has many other natural features, or **landforms**. Landforms can be different sizes and shapes. Plains are flat landforms on low ground. Along coasts, landforms such as peninsulas extend into the water. Valleys and canyons are also landforms. What other landforms can you name?

Some landforms take shape quickly, but others form over a long time. A mountain may take millions of years to form, but rocks rolling down its side can change the mountain in a hurry. Think about what happens to the large amounts of soil that a flood carries from one place to another. Or think about what happens to the dust that you may have seen blowing across an unplanted area on a windy day.

1. ✓**Checkpoint** Give two examples of changes to landforms.

2. How might rocks rolling down a mountain change other landforms too?

Weathering

Landforms change constantly. Some changes happen very slowly, so they are not easy to see. Before landforms can change, the rocks that form them must first break apart. **Weathering** is the process that breaks rocks in Earth's crust into smaller pieces. Water, ice, temperature changes, chemicals, and living things cause weathering.

Changes caused by weathering can be fast or very slow. Some changes take place in seconds. Sometimes you may notice changes after a few days or weeks. Other changes may take centuries. The two types of weathering are chemical weathering and physical weathering. You will read about physical weathering in Lesson 2.

Chemical Weathering

During chemical weathering, chemicals cause rocks to change into different materials and break down. Oxygen, carbon dioxide, and water mix with other materials in the air near Earth's surface. The substances that form when these materials mix can break into smaller pieces. For example, rainwater mixes with carbon dioxide in the air. It forms a weak acid. When the rain falls, the acid in it combines with the rock material on Earth's surface to form a new substance. The rock is slowly broken down. Pollution in the air can cause even more acid in the rain.

Acid rain weathers rock material on Earth's surface. It also changes rock used for buildings and monuments. You can see an example of how acid rain affects rock by looking at the pictures of Cleopatra's Needle.

Water and warm temperatures are important for chemical weathering. Areas that get a lot of rain have more chemical weathering than deserts have. Warm areas also have more chemical weathering than cold areas have.

Cleopatra's Needle had been slowly weathering in the Egyptian desert for about 3500 years.

In the late 1800s, the monument was moved to London, England. For about 125 years, acid rain in this cooler, wetter place has worn away the stone. Now you can barely see the markings.

Salt Point State Park

✓ **Lesson Review**

1. What is chemical weathering and how does it affect rocks?

2. ✏️ **Writing in Science**

   Descriptive Use the photos on pages 234 and 235 to describe how water is a part of chemical weathering.

Lesson 2

What causes physical weathering?

Natural forces on Earth also cause physical weathering. These forces slowly change the surface of Earth.

Physical Weathering

You read in Lesson 1 that chemical weathering causes rocks to change into different materials and break down. In physical weathering, rocks are broken into smaller pieces. But only the size of the rocks changes. The rocks do not change into new materials. Plants, ice, and water all cause physical weathering. When they work together, rock weathers even faster.

Have you ever seen a weed growing in a crack in the sidewalk? Weeds and other plants can also grow in cracks in rocks. As the plants and their roots grow, they split the soil and rocks. Roots break apart some rocks, such as granite, more slowly than other rocks, such as sandstone.

Glaciers can also cause physical weathering. Glaciers are huge moving sheets of ice that creep very slowly over land. As the glacier slides along, it drags rocks with it. The rocks scrape along the ground, forming valleys and ridges. The glacier also grinds rocks into smaller pieces.

This plant's root is breaking apart granite.

Physical weathering can cause rock to split into sheets.

Standards Focus 4ES5.0 Waves, wind, water, and ice shape and reshape Earth's land surface. As a basis for understanding this concept:
4ES5.b Students know natural processes, including freezing and thawing and the growth of roots, cause rocks to break down into smaller pieces.
4IE6.c Students will formulate and justify predictions based on cause-and-effect relationships.

236

Freezing and Thawing

Ice breaks rocks as well. When water freezes, it expands, or gets larger. Water from rain or melted snow seeps into cracks in rocks. As the water freezes, the ice pushes against the sides of the crack. This makes the crack deeper and wider. Each time this happens, the crack gets a little bit larger. In time, the rock will split.

Think of a soft plastic bottle that is completely filled with water. The bottle is tightly capped and placed in the freezer overnight. What do you predict will happen? The water expands and changes the shape of the bottle. Sometimes the bottle even splits! How does this show that freezing can cause physical weathering?

Cycles of freezing and thawing caused this rock to split.

1. **✓ Checkpoint** How does ice cause physical weathering?

2. Sometimes ice and plant roots affect the same rock. Explain how this can speed up the time it takes to break the rock.

Over millions of years, waves carrying sand and pebbles carved a hole in this cliff.

Water and Weathering

Look at the picture at the left. What do you think carved the hole through the rock? It was the water! The constant action of flowing water and waves shapes landforms along coasts. Sand and gravel in the waves act like sandpaper. As the waves crash against the rocks, the sand and gravel wear away the rocks. Then the broken pieces of rock, the sand, and the gravel all scrape against rock the waves hit. The weathering process continues.

Flowing water shapes landforms, too. Rivers carry pebbles, sand, mud, and other sediments. These sediments rub against the rock that makes up the riverbed. They slowly wear away the rock, leaving valleys and canyons. The picture below shows how flowing water carves a path through the land.

Sand, soil, and other sediment broke apart the rock as the river flowed.

Soil

As you have seen, the rocks at and beneath Earth's surface are affected by plants, ice, and water. Weathering breaks these rocks into tiny pieces. The little pieces of rock are ingredients in soil. **Soil** is the thin layer of loose, weathered material that covers most of the land surface of Earth. The pictures on the right show how scientists classify the pieces of rock that make up soil.

Most soil is made up of sand, silt, and clay. Soil also includes decaying plant and animal matter called humus. The exact combination is different for every kind of soil. Water and air fill in the spaces between particles of sand, silt, clay, and humus. The amount of each ingredient in the mixture determines what kinds of plants grow well in the soil.

Sizes of Rocks

Weathering breaks rocks into smaller and smaller pieces. Water wears many rocks to a smooth and rounded shape. The list shows the size of the pieces from largest to smallest.

Boulder 300 mm

Cobble 100 mm

Pebble 30 mm

Sand 1 mm

Silt Each is a tiny speck!

Clay You need a microscope to see clay particles clearly!

1. **✓ Checkpoint** What are three names scientists use to describe small pieces of rock that make up soil?

2. **Sequence** Show the sequence of weathering due to flowing water. Use a graphic organizer to help.

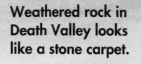

Weathered rock in Death Valley looks like a stone carpet.

More Weathering

Over time, some rock breaks into tiny pieces as it weathers. But what happens to the larger pieces? The larger weathered pieces are the fantastic shapes you see in the photos in this lesson. Huge arches, towers, and other shapes can be formed in this way. Notice how some of the weathered rocks look very smooth. Others seem to have sharp corners.

You can also see some smaller pieces of weathered rock. Some of the weathered rock may have been moved by the wind or other forces. First, blowing winds pick up tiny bits of sand, soil, or dust. When the particles blow against a rock, they scrape against it. Next tiny bits of the rock break off. Then these bits are blown away.

Pieces of rock and soil in open areas such as farm fields keep weathering. The top layer of soil, called topsoil, is the best kind of soil for growing crops.

These weathered rocks are in California's Alabama Hills.

Waves

You can see large pieces of weathered rock near the ocean too. Waves and flowing water break large rocks near the coast into smaller pieces of rock. The water and the wind carry away particles of rock, soil, and sand. The particles bump and scrape against each other and against other rock. Over time, they become smaller and smaller. Later, the water or the wind may deposit these tiny pieces in other places. You will read more about this process in Lesson 3.

✓**Lesson Review**

1. What are three causes of physical weathering?

2. How are physical weathering by flowing water and by ice different?

3. ✏ **Writing in Science** Descriptive
   Describe how flowing water slowly changes the land.

Lesson 3

How does weathered material move?

Many forces move weathered rock and deposit it in new places. The deposits slowly reshape Earth's surface.

Erosion

You have read that plants, ice, and water can break down rock. But what happens to the small pieces of rock? Sometimes the rock stays where it is. Sometimes it is picked up and carried to other places. **Erosion** is the movement of weathered materials. Wind, water, glaciers, living things, and gravity cause erosion.

These photos were taken less than one minute apart. The waves that caused the pillar to collapse now transport its pieces.

Transport

Water often carries, or **transports**, weathered materials from one place to another. Rain picks up loose material from rocks. The runoff from the rain flows into streams and rivers. The rivers carry rock from place to place. If the water slows down, some of the rock may settle. Rivers can make new land forms by carrying bits of rock and soil into the ocean! Moving water is the most important force in transporting weathered materials.

Wind and gravity can also transport material. When sand and soil are dry, wind can easily blow them to new places. Gravity pulls rocks and soil downhill. If the slope is gentle, the rocks and soil move slowly. But they can move quickly if the slope is steep.

Living things can move soil too. For example, ground squirrels tunnel through soil. Worms mix and move soil from one layer to another. Large tree roots grow through soil, pushing the soil aside. Air and water can move into and fill the empty spaces.

Standards Focus 4ES5.0 Waves, wind, water, and ice shape and reshape Earth's land surface. As a basis for understanding this concept:
4ES5.a Students know some changes in earth are due to slow processes, such as erosion, and some changes are due to rapid processes, such as landslides, volcanic eruptions, and earthquakes.
4ES5.c Students know moving water erodes landforms, reshaping the land by taking it away from some places and depositing it as pebbles, sand, silt, and mud in other places (weathering, transport, and deposition).

Rivers erode rocks and soil. They carry particles of sand, silt, mud, and clay to new places. This photograph shows the valleys that are carved through erosion. It also shows how rivers change landforms near the ocean.

1. **✓Checkpoint** Name four ways that eroded materials are transported.

2. **Writing in Science**
Descriptive Look at the photo on this page. Describe how water is reshaping the land by eroding the landforms.

Transport and Deposition

Pieces of rock and soil can be carried away by wind or flowing water. The pieces are removed from one place and transported to other places. As parts of Earth's surface are worn down, other parts are built up. **Deposition** is the laying down of pieces of rock and soil. Sometimes deposition happens slowly, and at other times it happens very quickly.

When the water flows quickly, it can carry large particles for great distances. As the moving water slows, the largest particles settle on the bottom first. Then smaller particles, such as sand, sink. Finally, the smallest bits of silt and clay sink too. Think about the pictures that show sediment deposited by rivers. These places are called deltas. Ocean waves also carry sand from one place to another. Sandy islands sometimes form along coasts. Erosion can move these islands from one place to another!

Wind can also erode, transport, and deposit small particles. Wind deposits silt and clay, which form a layer on top of the soil. In deserts, winds deposit grains of sand in large, loose piles called sand dunes. Without plants or barriers to keep the sand from blowing, wind continues to shape the dunes.

Glaciers transport and deposit rocks as well. As glaciers move, they pick up rocks of all sizes—even large boulders. When glaciers melt, they deposit the rocks and soil they carried. Ridges of broken rocks and soil outline the areas glaciers once covered. Even small glaciers can break rocks apart and transport large pieces for long distances.

This water looks muddy because of the silt it is transporting.

Rivers are building new landforms in Morro Bay in central California. You can see the areas where silt has been transported from the land and deposited near the shore.

✓ **Lesson Review**

1. How do erosion, transport, and deposition change landforms?

2. **Sequence** You find a pebble in the middle of a field. What sequence of natural events might bring a piece of the pebble to the ocean? Use a graphic organizer to help.

keyword:
deposition
code:
gr4p244

What causes rapid changes to landforms?

Forces above and below Earth's surface work to cause rapid changes to the crust.

Rapid Changes

You are watching the news on television. You see pictures of a hillside that has slid down a canyon wall, burying a road. In just a few moments, the canyon's landforms have changed dramatically. So far, you have read about ways that Earth's surface changes slowly. But changes to Earth can happen in just weeks, days, minutes, or even seconds! Now you will read about some rapid changes and what causes them. They are landslides, earthquakes, and volcanoes.

Gravity and Landslides

No part of Earth's surface is perfectly flat. The force of gravity pulls objects from higher places to lower places. It causes loose, weathered material to roll downhill. Bits of rock and soil may move slowly downhill a little at a time. Rock and soil can also move rapidly. Events such as heavy rains may loosen material on a steep slope. Gravity then pulls the loosened material downward and into piles at the bottom.

Many landslides happen along coasts.

Floods can cause loose rock and soil to slide downward.

Standards Focus 4ES5.a Students know some changes in earth are due to slow processes, such as erosion, and some changes are due to rapid processes, such as landslides, volcanic eruptions, and earthquakes.

The rapid downhill movement of a large amount of rock and soil is a **landslide.** Remember that freezing and thawing can loosen rock. Rock that loosens during the winter may slide down the slope in the spring.

As you see from the photos, landslides can cause a lot of damage. Buildings, cars, trees, and other objects are sometimes carried along with the sliding soil. Anything in the landslide's path can be buried in sliding mud. Often, landslides on hills ruin buildings and destroy roads and bridges. A large landslide can cover a large area.

A landslide caused this boulder to fall on a road in Topanga Canyon.

1. ✓**Checkpoint** How is a landslide different from other kinds of erosion and deposition?

2. ✏️ **Writing in Science Narrative** Find out more about a landslide that happened in your area or in another place that interests you. Write a news report that describes what happened.

247

Volcanoes

A volcano can rapidly change Earth's surface. Before a volcano forms, certain events happen far below Earth's surface. At 80 to 160 kilometers (50 to 100 miles) deep, very hot molten rock, called magma, forms as rock melts. Gases in the magma make it rise toward the surface. A **volcano** is a cone-shaped landform that forms at a weak spot in Earth's crust where magma reaches the surface.

Lava flows out of an erupting volcano.

The volcano erupts when magma reaches the surface. Magma flowing from a volcano is called lava. Lava is still very hot, perhaps more than 1100°C (2000°F).

Sometimes the pressure builds so much that the gases in the magma explode. Hot rocks, gases, and ash are forced out of the volcano's openings, called vents. Not all volcanic eruptions are violent though. The type of eruption depends on the temperature and the kind of magma. Sometimes, magma oozes upward and flows from the volcano.

Dormant and Active Volcanoes

A volcano that has not erupted for a long time is said to be dormant. Mount Lassen in the Cascade Mountains in California has been dormant since 1921. Scientists cannot predict when the next eruption will happen.

A volcano is extinct if scientists do not think it will erupt again. Mount Kenya in Africa is extinct. There are extinct volcanoes in many places around the world.

An active volcano has frequent eruptions or shows signs of future eruptions. For example, since Kilauea in Hawaii began its most recent eruption in 1983, it has never stopped erupting.

When a volcano erupts, the land around it can change rapidly. A bowl-shaped area, or crater, may form around the main vent. The lava and ash can spread over a wide area, reshaping the volcano and the land around it.

The last eruption of Lassen Peak was in 1921.

1. **✓Checkpoint** How do volcanoes affect the land around them?

2. What causes magma beneath a volcano to rise to the surface?

1. Before erupting in May 1980, Mount St. Helens was more than 2,950 meters (9,600 ft) high.

2. Deep inside, pressure was building in gases in the magma. On May 18, 1980, the volcano erupted.

3. The pressure from the hot magma blasted rocks, ash, and gases into the air.

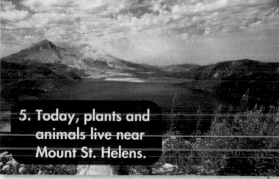

4. After the eruption, the volcano was 400 meters (1,314 ft) shorter.

5. Today, plants and animals live near Mount St. Helens.

Earthquakes may happen deep in Earth along fault lines. The surface of Earth shows the results of the shifting plates.

Earthquakes

Earth's outer layer, or crust, is on top of another layer called the upper mantle. Together, these two layers are divided into very large pieces called plates. The plates move all the time. Most earthquakes and volcanoes are along or near the places where Earth's plates meet.

A **fault** is a break or crack in rocks where Earth's crust can move. Sometimes, rocks along a fault can get stuck. The plates, however, continue their slow movement, or creep. They put pressure on the rocks. If the pressure becomes strong enough, the rocks will break, and the plates will move suddenly. The sudden movement that causes Earth's crust to shake is an **earthquake.** Like volcanoes, earthquakes can cause major, rapid changes to Earth's surface.

The vibrations of an earthquake move as waves that travel through Earth. Waves that travel along Earth's surface move back and forth and up and down. These waves can cause cracks in Earth's surface.

Earth's Crust Shaking

The changes in landforms that an earthquake causes depend on how close the earthquake is to the surface and how long the crust shakes or moves. Also, an earthquake will cause more damage near a town with many buildings than it would in a remote area. Many modern buildings are made so that they are less affected by earthquakes than older buildings are.

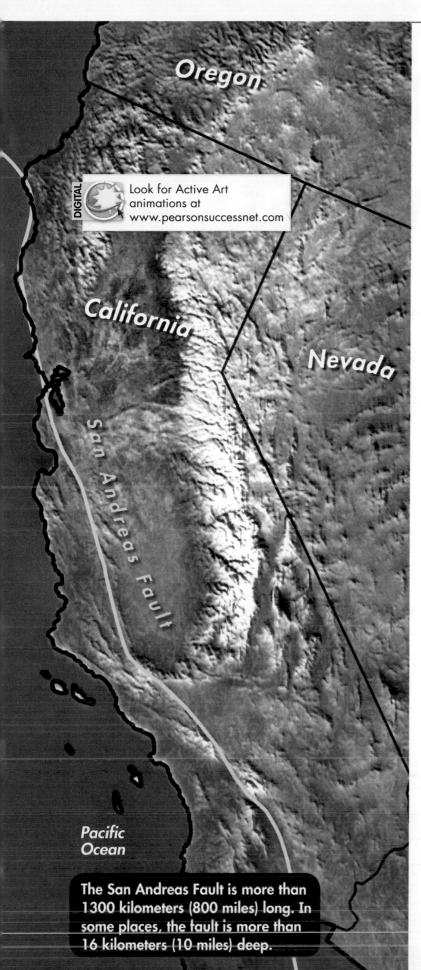

Oregon

California

Nevada

San Andreas Fault

Pacific
Ocean

Look for Active Art
animations at
www.pearsonsuccessnet.com

The San Andreas Fault is more than
1300 kilometers (800 miles) long. In
some places, the fault is more than
16 kilometers (10 miles) deep.

Plates Meeting

In California, many towns and cities are built along a huge fault system named the San Andreas Fault. Two plates meet along the San Andreas Fault. You can see in the photo where the two plates meet. The fault system runs from north to south through much of California. Many earthquakes happen near the fault.

Most earthquakes are small. You might feel a slight tremor or see the water in a fish bowl move. A few earthquakes are powerful enough to damage buildings, roads, and bridges. In 1906 and 1989, strong earthquakes broke gas lines in San Francisco. The broken gas lines caused fires. The fire in 1906 burned for three days and destroyed 500 city blocks.

Earthquakes can also cause landslides on the ocean floor or on land. Undersea landslides can form giant waves that may cause floods. The 1980 eruption of Mount St. Helens began moments after a landslide that was caused by an earthquake. As you have read, landslides can bury large areas and destroy buildings.

✓ Lesson Review

1. Name three ways that Earth's surface can change rapidly.

2. ✏️ **Writing in Science**
   Summarize What causes an earthquake?

Math in Science

Comparing Sizes of Earthquakes

One way to estimate the strength of an earthquake has to do with the size of the vibrations, or waves, that go out from the point underground where the earthquake begins. An earthquake scale is a way of comparing the size of these waves. The earthquake is given a number, usually between 0 and 10. This number, called the magnitude, depends on the size of the earthquake's waves.

STRONGEST EARTHQUAKES IN THE US, 1811–2002			
Earthquake	Location	Year	Approximate Magnitude
A	New Madrid, MO	1811	8.1
B	New Madrid, MO	1812	7.8
C	New Madrid, MO	1812	8.0
D	Fort Tejon, CA	1857	7.9
E	Imperial Valley, CA	1892	7.8
F	Yakutat Bay, AK	1899	8.0
G	Near Cape Yakataga, AK	1899	7.9
H	San Francisco, CA	1906	7.8
I	East of Shumagin Islands, AK	1938	8.2
J	Andreanof Islands, AK	1957	9.1
K	Prince William Sound, AK	1964	9.2
L	Rat Islands, AK	1965	8.7
M	Andreanof Islands, AK	1986	8.0
N	Gulf of Alaska, AK	1987	7.9
O	Gulf of Alaska, AK	1988	7.8
P	Andreanof Islands, AK	1996	7.9
Q	Denali Fault, AK	2002	7.9

1. Copy the number line below. Mark and label points A through Q to show the magnitude of each earthquake in the table. When two or more earthquakes have the same magnitude, write the letters above each other. The labeling for magnitude 7.8 has been done for you.

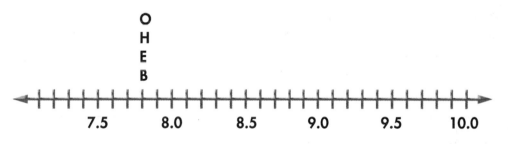

2. List the magnitudes from the table in order from least to greatest. Write each magnitude only once.

3. There were two big earthquakes in New Madrid, MO, in 1812. What was the magnitude of the stronger one?

4. What is the range of magnitudes listed? (Remember that the range is the difference between the greatest value and the least value.)

Lab zone Take-Home Activity

Refer to the table's dates. Make a table of the number of earthquakes that happened during each 10-year period. Begin with the period 1810–1819 and continue with 1820–1829 and so on, up to the present.

Investigate How can you observe erosion?

Materials

safety goggles

small paper cup and pencil

tub and spoon

sand, mud, rocks

eraser and ruler

graduated cylinder and water

What to Do

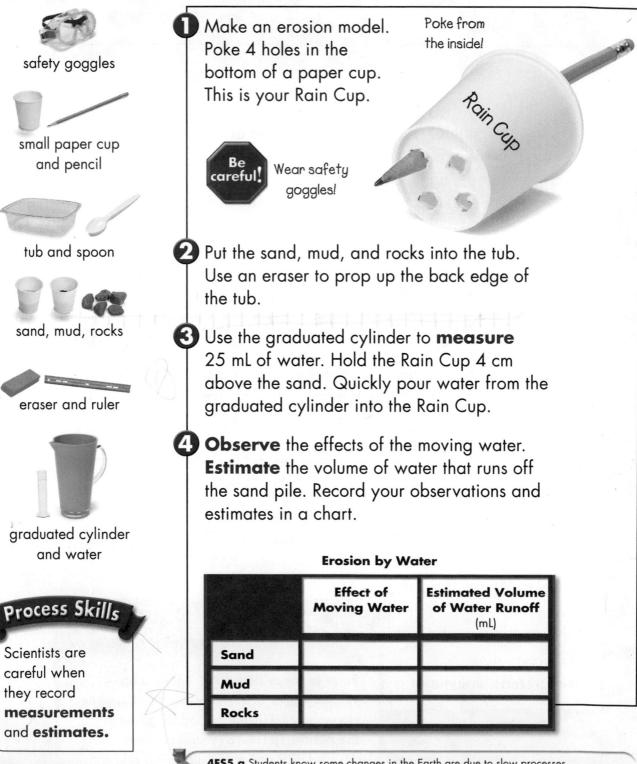

1 Make an erosion model. Poke 4 holes in the bottom of a paper cup. This is your Rain Cup.

Poke from the inside!

Rain Cup

Be careful! Wear safety goggles!

2 Put the sand, mud, and rocks into the tub. Use an eraser to prop up the back edge of the tub.

3 Use the graduated cylinder to **measure** 25 mL of water. Hold the Rain Cup 4 cm above the sand. Quickly pour water from the graduated cylinder into the Rain Cup.

4 **Observe** the effects of the moving water. **Estimate** the volume of water that runs off the sand pile. Record your observations and estimates in a chart.

Erosion by Water

	Effect of Moving Water	Estimated Volume of Water Runoff (mL)
Sand		
Mud		
Rocks		

4ES5.a Students know some changes in the Earth are due to slow processes, such as erosion, and some changes are due to rapid processes, such as landslides, volcanic eruptions, and earthquakes. **4IE6.b** Measure and estimate the weight, length, or volume of objects. (Also **4IE6.f**)

5 Repeat steps 3 and 4 for mud and rocks.

The eraser props up the back edge and makes the tub tilt forward.

Rain Cup

4 cm

sand pile
3 spoonfuls

mud pile
3 spoonfuls

rock pile
5 rocks

Explain Your Results

1. **Interpret Data.** Which was eroded the most, the sand, the mud pile, or the rocks? the least?

2. Based on your **estimates,** which pile showed the greatest volume of runoff? How does the volume of runoff relate to how much erosion occurred in your model?

Go Further

How could you change your model to prevent water erosion? Think of a way to solve the problem. Then use your model to test your solution.

Chapter 7 Reviewing Key Concepts

Weathering and erosion change Earth's surface. Some changes happen slowly, and some happen quickly.

Lesson 1

How does Earth's surface slowly change?
- A process called weathering slowly breaks down Earth's surface.
- Chemical weathering breaks rock down into smaller pieces. Chemical weathering causes rock to change into different materials.

Lesson 2

What causes physical weathering?
- Physical weathering does not change the materials in rocks.
- Plant roots and ice can cause rocks to split apart.
- Water carries small bits of rock that wear away larger rocks.

Lesson 3

How does weathered material move?
- Erosion happens when wind, water, and glaciers move rock from one place to another.
- Wind, water, glaciers, and living things transport and deposit rock in new places.

Lesson 4

What causes rapid changes to landforms?
- Landslides are downhill movements of rocks and soil.
- Volcanoes erupt when magma is forced out of openings onto Earth's surface.
- Earthquakes are a result of Earth's plates moving along a fault.

Cross-Curricular Links

English–Language Arts

Building Vocabulary

Look again at the main picture on pages 228–229. Find the terms **weathering**, **erosion**, and **deposition**. Write a paragraph about each term that tells how it might relate to the picture.

Mathematics

Temperature

The temperature of water is 48°C. The water is put in a freezer. The temperature of the water drops 4 degrees each hour. About how many hours would it take for the water to begin to freeze? Remember that water freezes at a temperature of 0°C.

History–Social Science

Rivers, Oceans, and Land

Find California's main rivers and coasts on a map. Make a presentation to your class to show how rivers and oceans have changed the land.

Challenge!

English–Language Arts

After a Volcano Erupts

How does a volcano affect the land right after an eruption? How does the land change in the years following an eruption? Use information you find in the library-media center to write a composition that describes the sequence of events that affect the land near the volcano.

Chapter 7 Review/Test

Use Vocabulary

deposition page 244	**landslide** page 247
earthquake page 250	**soil** page 239
erosion page 242	**transport** page 242
fault page 250	**volcano** page 248
landform page 233	**weathering** page 234

Fill in the blanks with the correct vocabulary words. If you have trouble answering a question, read the listed page again.

1. Underground rock suddenly shifts and Earth's crust shakes during a(n) _____.

2. Hot magma moves upward and erupts from a(n) _____.

3. Glaciers cause _____ by moving rocks and soil to new places.

4. A fan-shaped area near the mouth of a river may result from _____.

5. _____ occurs when acid in rainwater changes rock.

6. A mountain is one kind of _____.

Think About It

7. How does its size affect where a piece of rock is deposited by water?

8. How do the roots of plants cause weathering?

9. **Process Skills** **Infer** Many volcanoes are located near the Pacific Ocean—on the east coast of Asia and on the west coasts of North and South America. What can you infer about Earth's crust in these areas?

10. **Classify** each event as either weathering or erosion.
    a a river carrying silt to the ocean
    b ice freezing in a crack of a rock
    c mud sliding rapidly down a hill

11. **Sequence** Make a graphic organizer like the one below to show what happens in a landslide.

12. **Writing in Science**
    Narrative You are many kilometers from an active volcano. While you are watching, it suddenly erupts. Tell how the volcano looked before, during, and after the eruption.

California Standards Practice

Write the letter of the correct answer.

13. Plate movement along which of the following causes many earthquakes?

A fault

B landform

C slowly moving river

D rapidly flowing river

14. Which statement is true?

A Waves in the ocean cause erosion, but not deposition.

B Winds cause most landslides.

C Acid rain can cause earthquakes.

D Soil is formed from weathered rock.

15. Which of the following can cause physical weathering?

A ice

B deposition

C chemicals

D acid rain

16. Which word describes the rapid downhill movement of rock and soil caused by gravity?

A delta

B earthquake

C landslide

D volcano

17. Which results from deposition?

A a delta

B a valley

C a river

D a fault

18. Which describes weathering?

A It is caused only by living things.

B It results only from chemicals.

C It can happen slowly.

D It is often seen before earthquakes.

19. Why is wind erosion so common in deserts?

A Deserts are very moist.

B Deserts are very dry.

C Deserts are landforms.

D Deserts do not have minerals.

20. What might happen to the land shown in the drawing?

A a flood

B an earthquake

C transport

D erosion

Studying Earth's Water from Space

Earth is the only planet that we know has lots of liquid water. Its land, air, and oceans all interact. NASA has different ways of collecting data about Earth's water.

Tropical Rainfall Measuring Mission

The Tropical Rainfall Measuring Mission (TRMM) was launched in November 1997. Measurements from TRMM are used to find where rain is falling in the areas near Earth's equator. It also lets researchers know how hard it is raining in places without people nearby to measure the rain. It can even measure rain that falls from clouds but evaporates before it reaches the ground. This information helps researchers predict winds, ocean currents, and floods.

The winds in a cyclone circle around a center that has low pressure.

Aqua Satellite

Aqua is the Latin word for "water." The *Aqua* satellite was launched in May 2002. Its main goal is to gather information about water in Earth's system. The information will help scientists understand more about Earth's water cycle, the oceans, and our environment. *Aqua* carries six instruments. One of the instruments can measure ocean temperature accurately, even though clouds might cover the ocean. Measuring ocean temperature gives scientists important information about changes on Earth.

This *Aqua* satellite image shows waves near Indonesia.

ICESat

The *Ice, Cloud, and Land Elevation Satellite* was launched in January 2003. It uses lasers to measure ice sheets covering Antarctica and Greenland. It also uses the lasers to measure the altitudes of clouds, mountains, and forests. Scientists will use the measurements taken over several years to determine whether the ice sheets are melting or growing as Earth's climate changes.

Greenland's ice sheet is melting.

Lab zone Take-Home Activity

Set up a rain gauge at your home. Measure the rainfall for one month and make a chart to show your data.

Dr. Jean Dickey

Dr. Jean Dickey uses views of Earth from space to measure Earth's movements.

As a child growing up in Pennsylvania, Jean Dickey, like her mother, had a strong interest in math and science. While she was still in college, she worked at the Argonne National Laboratory. This laboratory does work in many areas of math and science.

Today, Dr. Dickey is a physicist at NASA's Jet Propulsion Laboratory. One of Dr. Dickey's recent projects was to investigate why Earth appears to be bulging around its middle. That's right! Earth is getting about 1 millimeter "fatter" near the equator each year. After much study, Dr. Dickey and others found two causes for Earth's "weight gain." One is the rapid melting of glaciers. Another is a change in the size and shape of Earth's oceans.

Dr. Dickey's group is also responsible for keeping an eye on Earth's movements in space. They measure and record even the smallest shifts in Earth's place in space. This information is used to help navigate spacecraft.

Lab zone Take-Home Activity

Draw and color a cartoon that shows what is happening to Earth around the equator. Include sentences that explain why it is getting larger.

Unit C Summary

Chapter 6

How are rocks and minerals formed?
- Scientists use properties such as color, hardness, luster, cleavage, streak, and crystal structure to identify minerals.
- Ores are rocks with minerals that can be removed from Earth's crust and used to make products.
- Igneous, sedimentary, and metamorphic rocks form in different ways.
- The rock cycle is a continuing process in which rocks can change into different kinds of rock.

Chapter 7

How is Earth's surface shaped and reshaped?
- Earth's surface slowly changes through the processes of physical and chemical weathering.
- Physical weathering is caused by the action of water, ice, glaciers, and living things.
- Weathered material moves from one place to another through the processes of erosion, transport, and deposition.
- Landslides, volcanoes, and earthquakes cause fast changes to Earth's surface.

Experiment What settles first?

Materials

3 small measuring cups

small gravel, sand, clay soil

plastic bottles with caps

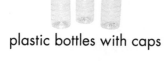

funnel and water

Process Skills

Experiments have a **variable** you change, a variable you **observe,** and variables you **control.**

Ask a question.
How do particles in water settle out?

State a hypothesis.
Do larger particles settle out faster, slower, or at about the same speed as smaller particles? Write your **hypothesis.**

Identify and control variables.
The **variable** you change is the size of the particles. The variable you observe is how fast the particles settle. Every other part of the experiment must be controlled, or kept the same.

gravel – largest particles
sand – medium-sized particles
clay soil – smallest particles

Control the amount of each type of particle. Use equal amounts of gravel, sand, and clay soil. Control how long the bottles are shaken. Shake all bottles the same length of time. Control when the particles start to settle. Stop shaking all bottles at the same time.

4ES5.c Student know moving water erodes landforms, reshaping the land by taking it away from some places and depositing it as pebbles, sand, silt, and mud in other places (weathering, transport, and deposition). **4IE6.d** Conduct multiple trials to test a prediction and draw conclusions about the relationships between predictions and results. (Also **4IE6.f)**

Test your hypothesis.

1 **Measure** 30 mL of gravel, 30 mL of sand, and 30 mL of clay soil.

2 Put each kind of particle into a different bottle. Use a funnel. Fill each bottle $\frac{3}{4}$ full with water.

Hint: If the funnel jams, tap it or shake it.

3 Screw the caps on tightly. Along with 2 others in your group, begin shaking the bottles.

(largest particles)

gravel

(medium-sized particles)

sand

(smallest particles)

clay soil

$\frac{3}{4}$ full with water

4 At the same time, stop shaking the bottles.
Put them on a table. Observe what happens.

gravel

sand

clay soil

5 Record the order the contents settle.

6 Repeat twice. Do a total of 3 trials.

Multiple Trials

Scientists usually conduct multiple trials. Multiple trials help make results more reliable. When scientists complete their investigations and experiments, they compare their results with their predictions and hypotheses.

Collect and record your data.

Type of Particles	Speed of Settling (fastest speed, medium speed, slowest speed)				
	Predicted	Trial A	Trial B	Trial C	Overall
Largest particles (small gravel)					
Medium-sized particles (sand)					
Smallest particles (clay soil)					

Interpret your data.

Analyze the information in your chart. Compare what you thought would happen with your results.

Why do you think scientists repeat experiments?

State your conclusion.

Draw a conclusion about the relationship between your hypothesis and your results. Does your conclusion agree with your hypothesis? **Communicate** your conclusion.

Go Further

What would happen if the soil had particles of different sizes mixed together? Make a **prediction** based on the results of this activity. Design and carry out a plan to investigate this or any other questions you have.

Show What You Know

Be a Rock Geologist

Collect rocks and classify them according to their characteristics and the minerals that form them. Write down your observations of color, luster, and cleavage. You might also include texture, that is how the rock feels when you touch it. Then classify the rocks as igneous, sedimentary, or metamorphic. Make a rock display. Record your observations for each type of rock on note cards. You may use a rock and mineral guide to help you identify the rocks.

Build a Landscape

Use clay, cardboard, and other materials to show an area with a variety of landforms. Be sure to include some of the landforms that you read about in Chapter 7. Then label each landform. Write a few sentences on a note card to describe how erosion, transport, and deposition may change it. Display the cards on your model.

Write Historical Fiction

Write a historical fiction story about an earthquake that took place in the United States. Write about the time and place of the earthquake. Describe what happened to the surrounding area during and after the earthquake. Remember that historical fiction tells a story about events that actually happened with fictional characters. Your story should include these elements:

- the events before, during, and after the earthquake.
- how the earthquake affected the characters in the story.
- a beginning, middle, and end.

Read More About Earth Sciences

Look for other books about Earth Sciences in your library–media center. One book you may want to read is:

Planet Earth/Inside Out
by Gail Gibbons

This book describes some of the forces that are constantly changing the shape of Earth's landforms. It shows the layers of Earth and the huge plates that form the crust. It also shows examples of different kinds of rock.

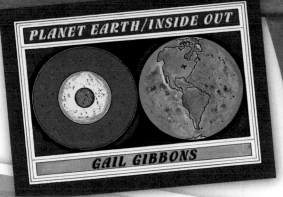

Science Fair Projects

Full Inquiry

Using Scientific Methods

1. Ask a question.
2. State a hypothesis.
3. Identify and control variables.
4. Test your hypothesis.
5. Collect and record your data.
6. Interpret your data.
7. State your conclusion.
8. Go further.

Does acid rain affect rock?

Many buildings and statues are made from rock. Acid rain is a weak acid.

Idea: Prepare several cups with different strengths of vinegar and water mixtures. Place a piece of chalk in each cup of water. (Vinegar is an acid.) After 24 hours, compare the pieces of chalk. Test other materials people use for buildings.

Does ice affect rock?

Water freezing into ice weathers rock.

Idea: Fill a drinking straw with water. Seal the ends of the straw with modeling clay. Freeze the straw. Write a hypothesis describing what you predict will happen. The next day, remove the straw from the freezer. Write a summary to explain what happened and why. Test straws filled with salt water or other liquids.

How do soil samples differ?

Soil is a combination of materials. The amount of each material affects the properties of the soil.

Idea: Collect soil samples from your area. Use a magnifier to identify how much of each sample is sand, silt, and clay. Write a hypothesis predicting which will hold the most water. Then test the flow of water through each sample.

Unit C California Standards Practice

Write the letter of the correct answer.

1. **A rock that has uneven layers of minerals is probably which kind of rock?**

   A an ore

   B igneous

   C sedimentary

   D metamorphic

2. **Which is the correct sequence of the processes that resulted in the fan-shaped landform shown in the picture?**

   A erosion, deposition, transport

   B erosion, layering, weathering

   C transport, weathering, erosion

   D erosion, transport, deposition

3. **A sedimentary rock is exposed to heat and pressure. What type of rock will form?**

   A ore

   B igneous

   C sedimentary

   D metamorphic

4. **Which of these is probably the result of erosion caused by flowing water?**

   A a mountain

   B a valley

   C a glacier

   D a fault line

5. **An igneous rock has very large interlocking crystals. How did the rock most likely form?**

   A It cooled slowly and hardened.

   B It cooled quickly and hardened.

   C It was formed by deposition.

   D It was formed from sediments.

Unit C California Standards Practice

6. Which of the following can change Earth's surface as a result of the force of gravity?

A wind

B ice

C landslides

D plant roots

7. The picture shows how roots can affect rock. What other natural process of weathering can force rock to split apart?

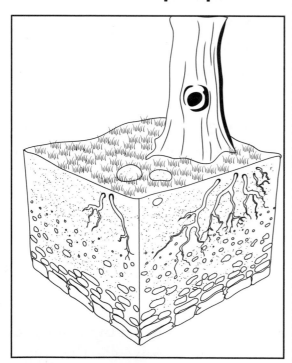

A water freezing

B chemical weathering

C wind erosion

D rock cycling

8. When magma cools and hardens, which type of rock does it form?

A metamorphic

B igneous

C sedimentary

D fragmented

9. What is the process by which rocks change into other kinds of rock called?

A erosion

B the rock cycle

C a fault

D transport

10. Which is an example of a lead ore?

A copper

B hornblende

C galena

D hematite

11. A scientist finds hematite in a group of rocks. Which is the best conclusion the scientist can make?

A Fossils will be found in layers.

B The rocks contain iron.

C The ore will contain no crystals.

D Gold flakes will be found in the ore.

Unit C California Standards Practice

12. During deposition, which of the following would most likely be the first particles to settle at the bottom of a river?

  A clay

  B pebbles

  C sand

  D silt

13. Which of the following causes chemical weathering?

  A rainwater that mixes with oxygen

  B rainwater that freezes and thaws

  C rainwater that mixes with carbon dioxide

  D rainwater that contains particles of silt or clay

14. Which of the following probably caused the hole in this rock?

  A erosion by wind

  B erosion by waves

  C deposition by ice

  D weathering by rain

15. Which of the following slowly transports rocks of all sizes over large areas on Earth?

  A landslides

  B earthquakes

  C volcanoes

  D glaciers

16. Which place is the most likely site of an earthquake?

  A where magma builds up

  B at fault lines

  C where metamorphic rocks are formed

  D at deposits of clay, silt, and pebbles

17. Which of the following is an example of a slow change to Earth's surface?

  A earthquake

  B erupting volcano

  C landslide

  D weathering

18. Which of the following is the most common way that an earthquake changes landforms?

  A It wears away rock.

  B It spreads lava over a wide area.

  C It scrapes out new valleys.

  D It shifts the land.

Unit C California Standards Practice

19. A mineral is black and has a rank of 6 on the Mohs scale. It has a silky luster. Use the mineral information table to identify the mineral.

- **A** hornblende
- **B** hematite
- **C** galena
- **D** magnetite

20. A dark-colored sample of a mineral can be scratched with a copper penny. Use the mineral information table to identify this sample.

- **A** calcite
- **B** feldspar
- **C** mica
- **D** quartz

Mineral	Hardness	Luster	Streak	Color	Other
Calcite	3	ranges from glassy to dull	white	one color, ranging from colorless to white, pink, yellow, greenish, red	fizzes when vinegar is poured on it
Feldspar	6–6.5	glassy or pearly	white	colorless or many colors, including beige, pink, grey, bluish-green	group of Earth's most common minerals
Galena	2.5	metallic	gray	lead-gray	heavy for its size
Hematite	5–6	metallic or nonmetallic	reddish brown	silver-gray or red	feels grainy
Hornblende	5–6	silky	pale gray to gray	dark-green to black	often has long, dark crystals; cleavage in 2 directions
Magnetite	5.5–6	shiny, metallic	black	black	magnetic
Mica	2–2.5	pearly	white	dark brown, black, silver-white	flakes when peeled
Quartz	7	glassy	white	clear (may be colored by impurities)	fractures along curved surfaces, like broken glass

Mineral	Hardness
Talc	1
Gypsum	2
Fingernail: 2.5	
Calcite	3
Copper penny: 3.0	
Fluorite	4
Apatite	5
Glass: 5.5	
Feldspar	6
Steel file: 6.5	
Quartz	7
Topaz	8
Corundum	9
Diamond	10

CALIFORNIA

California Science Content Standards, Grade 4

STANDARD SET 1. Physical Sciences

4PS1.0 Electricity and magnetism are related effects that have many useful applications in everyday life. As a basis for understanding this concept:

4PS1.a Students know how to design and build simple series and parallel circuits by using components such as wires, batteries, and bulbs.	pp. **16, 17, 20, 21, 22, 23, 28, 29,** 30, 32, 33, 75, 80, 83, 84, 85
4PS1.b Students know how to build a simple compass and use it to detect magnetic effects, including Earth's magnetic field.	pp. 48, 49, **50, 51, 52, 53,** 70, 72, 73, 75, 85, 86
4PS1.c Students know electric currents produce magnetic fields and know how to build a simple electromagnet.	pp. 43, 44, 45, **54,** 55, **56, 57, 68, 69, 70,** 72, 73, 75, **76, 77, 78, 79,** 84
4PS1.d Students know the role of electromagnets in the construction of electric motors, electric generators, and simple devices, such as doorbells and earphones.	pp. 58, 59, **60, 61, 62, 63, 64, 65,** 70, 72, 73, 84, 85
4PS1.e Students know electrically charged objects attract or repel each other.	pp. **6, 9, 10,** 11, 12, **13, 30,** 32, **75,** 84, 86
4PS1.f Students know that magnets have two poles (north and south) and that like poles repel each other while unlike poles attract each other.	pp. **40, 43, 44,** 45, **46, 47,** 51, 70, 72, 75, 81, 85, 86
4PS1.g Students know electrical energy can be converted to heat, light, and motion.	pp. 14, **15, 18, 19, 30,** 32, 33, 75, 83, 85

What It Means to You

Electricity and magnetism play a huge role in our lives. If you've ever gotten a "shock" by touching a metal doorknob, you've felt a tiny electric charge. Electric charges can build up during a storm and cause lightning. Electric current is formed when electric charges move through wires. Electric current in circuits can be changed to heat food, light a room, or spin a CD. Magnetic fields caused by electric current are used in electromagnets. You use electromagnets when you ring a doorbell, use a motor, or use a generator. Magnetic fields in magnets can be used to make a compass and detect Earth's magnetic field.

California Science Content Standards, Grade 4

STANDARD SET 2. Life Sciences

4LS2.0 All organisms need energy and matter to live and grow. As a basis for understanding this concept:

4LS2.a Students know plants are the primary source of matter and energy entering most food chains.	pp. **95,** 96, 97, **98,** 99, 114, **116,** 177, 185, 187
4LS2.b Students know producers and consumers (herbivores, carnivores, omnivores, and decomposers) are related in food chains and food webs and may compete with each other for resources in an ecosystem.	pp. **96, 97, 98,** 100, 101, 114, **115, 116,** 117, **150,** 151, 152, 153, 154, 155, 177, 185, 187, 188
4LS2.c Students know decomposers, including many fungi, insects, and microorganisms, recycle matter from dead plants and animals.	pp. 96, 101, **102, 103,** 104, 105, 106, 112, 113, 114, **116, 117,** 177, 188

What It Means to You

All living things need energy and matter to live and grow. You get energy by eating food that comes from plants and animals. In an ecosystem, energy passes from one organism to another by means of food chains and food webs. The energy flow starts with plants. They are called producers because they use matter from soil and energy from sunlight to produce food. Animals are consumers. They eat, or consume, plants or other animals. When plants and animals die or leave wastes, decomposers take over. They break down those materials and recycle them to the soil. Then plants can use the materials to make food. The pattern keeps repeating.

California Science Content Standards, Grade 4

STANDARD SET 3. Life Sciences

4LS3.0 Living organisms depend on one another and on their environment for survival. As a basis for understanding this concept:

4LS3.a Students know ecosystems can be characterized by their living and nonliving components.	pp. 100, 122, 124, **125,** 126, 127, 134, 135, 136, 137, 138, 139, **140,** 142, 143, 177, 185
4LS3.b Students know that in any particular environment, some kinds of plants and animals survive well, some survive less well, and some cannot survive at all.	pp. **126,** 127, 128, 129, 130, 131, 132, 133, 141, 148, **156,** 157, 158, 159, 170, 171, 172, 174, 175, 177, 178, 179, 180, 181, 186, 187, 188
4LS3.c Students know many plants depend on animals for pollination and seed dispersal, and animals depend on plants for food and shelter.	pp. 94, 96, 153, **158,** 160, 161, **162,** 163, **164,** 165, **166,** 167, 172, 174, 175, 177, 182, 186
4LS3.d Students know that most microorganisms do not cause disease and that many are beneficial.	pp. **106, 107, 108, 109,** 114, 115, 116, 117, 177, 185

What It Means to You

You live in an ecosystem. Your ecosystem provides you with food, water, and shelter. All ecosystems have living and nonliving parts that work together. Some nonliving resources of an ecosystem are air, water, and soil. Organisms survive only in ecosystems that provide the resources they need. Plants and animals have special body parts that help them meet their needs in their ecosystems. Plants in an ecosystem provide food and shelter for animals. Animals help some kinds of plants survive. They carry seeds to places where the seeds will have more room to grow.

California Science Content Standards, Grade 4

STANDARD SET 4. Earth Sciences (Rocks and Minerals)

4ES4.0 The properties of rocks and minerals reflect the processes that formed them. As a basis for understanding this concept:

4ES4.a Students know how to differentiate among igneous, sedimentary, and metamorphic rocks by referring to their properties and methods of formation (the rock cycle).	pp. **208, 209, 210,** 211 **212,** 213, **214, 215, 216, 217,** 222, 223, 224, 225, 263, 271, 272
4ES4.b Students know how to identify common rock-forming minerals (including quartz, calcite, feldspar, mica, and hornblende) and ore minerals by using a table of diagnostic properties.	pp. 194, 197, 198, **199,** 200, 201, 202, 203, 204, 205, **206, 207, 220, 221,** 224, 225, 268, 272, 274

What It Means to You

Earth is a rocky planet. We use rocks for making buildings, roads, and many other things. Above and below Earth's surface, three main types of rocks are continually being formed and changed. Igneous rocks are hard and sometimes have large crystals. Sedimentary rocks form in layers. Metamorphic rocks are hard and often have layers. Rocks are made of minerals. Each mineral has special properties, so each mineral can be used in a different way. Ores are rocks that contain large amounts of useful minerals. Hematite is a mineral that is found in an ore. Hematite is used for making iron and steel.

California Science Content Standards, Grade 4

STANDARD SET 5. Earth Sciences (Waves, Wind, Water, and Ice)

4ES5.0 Waves, wind, water, and ice shape and reshape Earth's land surface. As a basis for understanding this concept:

4ES5.a Students know some changes in the earth are due to slow processes, such as erosion, and some changes are due to rapid processes, such as landslides, volcanic eruptions, and earthquakes.	pp. 238, **246, 247, 248,** 249, **250,** 251, 252, 253, 254, 255, 256, 257, 258, 259, 263, 272, 273, 274
4ES5.b Students know natural processes, including freezing and thawing and the growth of roots, cause rocks to break down into smaller pieces.	pp. 230, 233, 234, 235, **236, 237,** 239, 240, 241, 256, 257, 258, 259, 263, 272, 273
4ES5.c Students know moving water erodes landforms, reshaping the land by taking it away from some places and depositing it as pebbles, sand, silt, and mud in other places (weathering, transport, and deposition).	pp. 233, **238, 239,** 240, 241, **242,** 243, **244,** 245, 256, 257, 258, 259, 263, 264, 265, 266, 267, 271, 273, 274

What It Means to You

You might have been frightened when you heard about landslides, volcanoes, and earthquakes. Those events changed parts of Earth's surface quickly. Other processes happen much more slowly, but they go on continually. Earth's surface changes all the time. Water, chemicals, temperature changes, and living things break down rocks. Wind, water, and gravity carry away rocky materials and deposit them in different places. As rocky materials are removed and deposited, the shapes of landforms change. Landforms that become eroded get smaller. Areas that receive deposited materials get larger.

California Science Content Standards, Grade 4

STANDARD SET 6. Investigation and Experimentation

4IE6.0 Scientific progress is made by asking meaningful questions and conducting careful investigations. As a basis for understanding this concept and addressing the content in the other three strands, students should develop their own questions and perform investigations. Students will:

4IE6.a Differentiate observation from inference (interpretation) and know scientists' explanations come partly from what they observe and partly from how they interpret their observations.	pp. **40, 92, 122,** 170, **171**
4IE6.b Measure and estimate the weight, length, or volume of objects.	pp. **68,** 69, 77, **136,** 179, **230, 254, 255**
4IE6.c Formulate and justify predictions based on cause-and-effect relationships.	pp. **28, 29,** 68, **69, 148**
4IE6.d Conduct multiple trials to test a prediction and draw conclusions about the relationships between predictions and results.	pp. **69, 78,** 79, **266, 267**
4IE6.e Construct and interpret graphs from measurements.	pp. **69,** 137
4IE6.f Follow a set of written instructions for a scientific investigation.	pp. **6, 28, 29, 40, 68, 69, 76, 77, 78, 79, 92, 112, 113, 122, 136, 137, 148, 170, 171, 178, 179, 180, 181, 194, 220, 221, 230, 254, 255, 264, 265, 266, 267**

What It Means to You

How does a simple motor work? You can investigate and solve such questions. You use your observations to make inferences. For instance, after observing many small bones and fur in a dissected owl pellet, you infer that owls eat small, furry animals such as mice. You use measurements to compare changes, such as the mass of chalk before and after weathering. A graph is a good way to show patterns that help explain cause-and-effect relationships used to make predictions. You test predictions many times before drawing conclusions. Written instructions keep your investigations organized and complete.

Glossary

The glossary uses letters and signs to show how words are pronounced. The mark ′ is placed after a syllable with a primary or heavy accent. The mark ′ is placed after a syllable with a secondary or lighter accent.

To hear these words pronounced, listen to the AudioText CD.

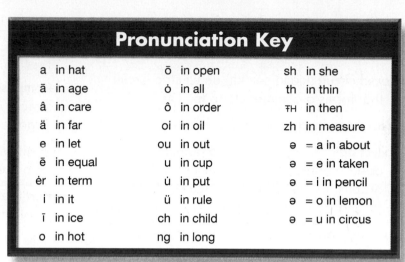

Pronunciation Key

a in hat	ō in open	sh in she
ā in age	ȯ in all	th in thin
â in care	ô in order	ᵺ in then
ä in far	oi in oil	zh in measure
e in let	ou in out	ə = a in about
ē in equal	u in cup	ə = e in taken
ėr in term	u̇ in put	ə = i in pencil
i in it	ü in rule	ə = o in lemon
ī in ice	ch in child	ə = u in circus
o in hot	ng in long	

acid rain (as′id rān) rainwater that combines with compounds in the air to form a weak acid (p. 234)

adaptation (ad′ap tā′shən) a trait that helps an organism survive in its environment (p. 156)

algae (al′jē) living things that usually live in water and can make their own food but do not have true leaves, stems, or roots like plants; singular alga (p. 106)

antibiotic (an′ti bī ot′ik) a substance produced by molds and bacteria that attacks harmful microorganisms (p. 107)

arch (ärch) a landform that looks like part of a loop (p. 240)

attract (ə trakt′) to be pulled toward each other (p. 9)

bacteria (bak tir′ē ə) simple one-celled living things; singular bacterium (p. 96)

baleen (bə lēn′) the bony plates in the mouth of a whale that trap tiny organisms as the whale squeezes the seawater out of its mouth (p. 157)

battery (bat′ər ē) an energy source that causes electric charges to flow (p. 16)

biomass (bī′ō mas′) the living matter in an area (p. 98)

boulder ((bōl′dər) a very large rock (p. 239)

calcite (kal′sīt) a mineral that can be colorless, white, or other pale colors and has a pearly luster (p. 197)

canopy (kan′ə pē) the top level of a rain forest, formed by tree branches, leaves, and vines tangled together (p. 130)

canyon (kan′yən) a landform similar to a valley with steep sides (p. 233)

carbon dioxide (kär′bən dī ok′sīd) a gas made of carbon and oxygen particles (p. 95)

carnivore (kär′nə vôr) an animal that eats other animals (p. 96)

cause (kȯz) why something happens (p. 7)

cause and effect why an event happens and what happens as a result of the event (p. 7)

chemical weathering (kem′ə kəl weᵺ′ər ing) the process of rock changing into new material and breaking down (p. 234)

classify (klas′ə fī) to arrange or sort objects, events, or living things according to their properties (p. xii)

cleavage (klē′vij) property of minerals that break along smooth, flat surfaces (p. 200)

climate (klī′mit) the average weather conditions in an area over a long time (p. 125)

closed circuit (klōzd sėr′kit) an electric circuit that forms a complete loop (p. 14)

coast (kōst) land bordered by the ocean (p. 233)

collect data (kə lekt′ dā′tə) to gather facts, observations, and measurements into graphs, tables, charts, or labeled diagrams (p. 79)

communicate (ke myü′nə kāt) to share ideas or information using words, pictures, graphs, tables, charts, and labeled diagrams (p. 79)

community (kə myü′nə tē) all of the different populations in one place (p. 151)

compare and contrast (kəm pâr′ and kən trast′) to show how things are alike and how they are different (p. 195)

compass (kum′pəs) an instrument that has a magnetic needle that points north (p. 48)

competition (kom′pə tish′ən) two or more living things using the same limited resources (p. 151)

conductor (kən duk′tər) a material that has low resistance and allows electricity to flow easily (p. 15)

consumer (kən sü′mər) a living thing that eats other living things for food (p. 96)

copper (kop′ər) a soft metal that is a good conductor and is easy to shape, often to make wire (p. 14)

coral reef (kôr′əl rēf) a ridge or mound in warm, shallow ocean waters formed by the skeletons of tiny sea animals called coral polyps (p. 132)

creep (krēp) the slow movement of rock or ice (p. 250)

crust (krust) the layer of rock that forms the outer surface of Earth (p. 233)

crystal (kris′tl) a three-dimensional shape with flat surfaces (p. 197)

decomposer (dē′kəm pō′zər) an organism that breaks down wastes and remains of other organisms (p. 96)

deposition (dep′ə zish′ən) the laying down of pieces of rock and soil (p. 244)

desert (dez′ərt) an ecosystem that receives very little precipitation (p. 128)

details (di tālz′) individual pieces of information that support a main idea (p. 41)

diatom (dī′ə tom) a kind of alga that has a hard cell wall (p. 106)

disease (də zēz′) sickness (p. 107)

dormant (dôr′mənt) in a state of rest (p. 249)

earthquake (ėrth′kwāk′) a sudden movement that causes Earth's crust to shake (p. 250)

ecosystem (ē′kō sis′təm) the living and nonliving things and the ways they interact in an environment (p. 95)

effect (ə fekt′) what happens as the result of a cause (p. 7)

electric charge (i lek′trik chärj) a property of some parts of matter, described as positive or negative (p. 9)

electric current (i lek′trik kėr′ənt) electric charges in motion (p. 14)

electric motor (i lek′trik mō′tər) a device that uses magnets to change electrical energy into motion (p. 62)

electrical circuit (i lek′trə kəl sėr′kit) a path that controls the direction of the flow of electric charges (p. 14)

electrical energy (i lek′trə kəl en′ər jē) the kind of energy in electrons or other charged objects (p. 17)

electricity (i lek′tris′ə tē) the kind of energy in electrically charged objects (p. 19)

electromagnet (i lek′trō mag′nit) a coil of wire through which electric current passes, creating a magnetic field (p. 56)

electron (i lek′tron) the part of an atom with a negative charge (p. 9)

environment (en vī′rən mənt) everything that surrounds a living thing (p. 95)

erosion (i rō′zhən) the movement of weathered materials (p. 242)

eruption (i rup′shən) an explosion of rock, gases, ash, and lava from a volcano (p. 248)

estimate (es′tə māt) to tell what you think an object's measurements are (p. xii)

euglena (yü glē′nə) a kind of protist, usually green, that lives in fresh water (p. 106)

experiment (ek sper′ə ment) to use scientific methods to test a hypothesis (p. 76)

explore (ek splôr′) to study a scientific idea in a hands-on manner (p. 6)

fault (fôlt) a break or crack where Earth's crust can move (p. 250)

feldspar (feld′spär′) a common rock-forming mineral with crystals that have sharp edges (p. 197)

fertilization (fer′tl ə zā′shən) the process by which an egg cell and a sperm cell combine (p. 165)

filament (fil′ə mənt) a very thin coiled wire in a light bulb that gets very hot and gives off light but does not melt (p. 18)

flood (flud) water level that is higher than usual and covers land that is usually dry (p. 246)

follow instructions (fol′ō in struk′shəns) to complete a task according to a given set of directions (p. 93)

food chain (füd chān) the transfer of energy and matter from one living thing to another by eating and being eaten (p. 98)

food web (füd web) a system of overlapping food chains in which energy and matter flow through many branches (p. 100)

freshwater (fresh′wô′tər) water that is not salty, usually found in lakes and rivers (p. 106)

fruit (früt) the part of a plant that contains the seeds (p. 165)

fungus (fung′gəs) a plant-like organism with no flowers or leaves; plural fungi (p. 96)

galena (gə lē′nə) a mineral ore that contains lead (p. 204)

generator (jen′ə rā′tər) a machine that uses moving magnets to produce electrical energy (p. 64)

glacier (glā′shər) a huge moving sheet of ice (p. 236)

grassland (gras′land′) an ecosystem that is covered with grasses but has few trees (p. 126)

ground (ground) the third prong of a plug that carries any extra electric current (p. 25)

habitat (hab′ə tat) an area or place where an organism lives in an ecosystem (p. 105)

hardness (härd′nes) a measure of how easily a mineral can be scratched (p. 199)

harmful (härm′fəl) causing damage (p. 107)

heat (hēt) the transfer of thermal energy between matter of different temperatures (p. 18)

hematite (hem′ə tīt) a mineral ore that contains iron (p. 199)

herbivore (ėr′bə vôr) an animal that eats plants (p. 96)

hornblende (hôrn′blend′) a common rock-forming mineral that breaks along flat, smooth surfaces (p. 199)

host (hōst) an organism that is harmed by a parasite (p. 152)

humus (hyü′məs) the decaying plant and animal matter in soil (p. 239)

hypothesis (hī poth′ə sis) a statement of one possible way to solve a problem or answer a question (p. 76)

identify and control variables (ī den′tə fī and kən trōl′ vâr′ ē ə bəlz) change one thing, but keep all the other factors the same (p. 76)

igneous (ig′nē əs) type of rock that forms from molten rock (p. 208)

infer (in fėr′) to draw a conclusion or make a reasonable guess based on what you have learned or what you know (p. 6)

insect (in′sekt) a small animal that has six legs and no backbone (p. 96)

instruction (in struk′shən) information or direction on how to do something (p. 93)

insulator (in′sə lā′tər) a material with so much resistance that it stops the flow of electric charges (p. 15)

interpret data (in tėr′prit dā′tə) to use the information you have collected to solve problems or answer questions (p. 79)

investigate (in ves′tə gāt) to solve a problem or answer a question by following a new or an existing procedure (p. 28)

iron (ī′ərn) a strong metal that is attracted by magnets and is used to make steel (p. 44)

landform (land′fôrm′) natural feature of Earth (p. 233)

landslide (land′slīd′) the rapid downhill movement of a large amount of rock and soil (p. 247)

lava (lä′və) hot, molten rock that reaches Earth's surface (p. 208)

lead (led) a dense blue-gray metal (p. 204)

light (līt) a kind of energy that can be seen and is used by plants to make food (p. 18)

luster (lus′tər) property of a mineral that describes how it reflects light (p. 198)

magma (mag′mə) hot, molten rock that forms deep underground (p. 208)

magnet (mag′nit) something that attracts iron and certain other metals (p. 44)

magnetic field (mag net′ik fēld) the space around a magnet in which magnetic forces operate (p. 44)

magnetic poles (mag net′ik pōlz) the two ends of a magnet, called the north magnetic pole and the south magnetic pole (p. 44)

magnetism (mag′nə tiz′ əm) a force that acts on either a moving electric charge or a magnetic material that is near a magnet (p. 43)

main idea (mān ī dē′ ə) the most important idea in a passage (p. 41)

main idea and details (mān ī dē′ ə and di tālz′) the most important piece of information and the smaller pieces that explain it (p. 41)

mammal (mam′əl) an animal that bears live young and has fur or hair (p. 155)

mantle (man′tl) the layer of Earth between the crust and the core (p. 250)

marine (mə rēn′) having to do with the ocean (p. 132)

marsh (märsh) a type of wetland where trees cannot grow (p. 156)

matter (mat′ər) anything that takes up space and has mass (p. 98)

measure (mezh′ər) to use a tool to find out how much of something there is, or how long or heavy an object is (p. 68)

mechanical energy (mə kan′ ə kəl en′ ər jē) energy of motion (p. 62)

metamorphic (met′ə môr′fik) type of rock formed when heat and pressure change the properties of rock (p. 212)

mica (mī′kə) a common rock-forming mineral that breaks into thin flakes (p. 197)

microorganism (mī′krō ôr′gə niz′əm) a living thing too small to be seen without a microscope (p. 104)

migrate (mī′grāt) to move from one place to another with the change of seasons (p. 156)

mineral (min′ər əl) a natural, nonliving, solid crystal that makes up rocks (p. 197)

model (mod′l) a sketch, diagram, or object that represents something that is difficult to observe directly and can be used to make predictions (p. 122)

Mohs scale (mōz skāl) a way of ranking how hard a mineral is (p. 199)

mold (mōld) a type of fungus (p. 105)

motion (mō′shən) changes in the position of an object over time (p. 18)

nectar (nek′tər) a sweet liquid made by flowers (p. 164)

nematode (nem′ə tōd) a roundworm (p. 108)

neutral (nü′trəl) neither positive nor negative (p. 9)

nitrogen (nī′trə jən) a gas that makes up most of the atmosphere (p. 98)

nutrient (nü′trē ənt) something an organism needs to perform its life processes (p. 95)

observe (əb zėrv′) to use your senses to find out about objects, events, or living things (p. 6)

omnivore (om′nə vôr′) an animal that eats both plants and animals (p. 96)

open circuit (ō′pən sėr′kit) an electric circuit that has at least one break (p. 14)

ore (ôr) a rock rich in valuable minerals that can be removed from Earth's crust (p. 202)

organism (ôr′ gə niz′əm) a living thing with parts that work together to carry on the processes of life (p. 96)

oxygen (ok′sə jən) a gas animals need to live (p. 95)

parallel circuit (par′ə lel sėr′kit) a circuit with two or more paths through which electric current can flow (p. 22)

parasite (par′ə sīt) an organism that lives on or in another organism, helping itself but hurting the other organism (p. 152)

pebble (peb′əl) a little, rounded rock (p. 239)

peninsula (pə nin′sə lə) a landform that extends out into the ocean (p. 233)

photosynthesis (fō′tō sin′thə sis) the process of plants using sunlight to make their own food (p. 95)

physical weathering (fiz′ə kəl weᴛн′ər ing) the process of rock breaking down into smaller pieces of the same material (p. 236)

pistil (pis′tl) a female structure in plants (p. 164)

plains (plānz) flat landforms on low ground (p. 233)

plankton (plangk′tən) tiny organisms that float in water (p. 157)

pollination (pol′ə nā′shən) the movement of pollen from a male part of a flower to a female part (p. 158)

pollution (pə lü′shən) any harmful waste in the environment (p. 234)

population (pop′yə lā′shən) all of the same kind of living things that live in one place (p. 151)

predator (pred′ə tər) a consumer that hunts other animals for food (p. 99)

predict (pri dikt′) to tell what you think will happen (p. 28)

pressure (presh′ər) a force applied to a substance and spread out over an area (p. 212)

prey (prā) an animal hunted by others for food (p. 99)

primary consumer (prī′mer′ē kən sü′mər) the living thing that eats the producer in a food chain (p. 98)

process (pros′es) changes that take place in a certain order (p. 95)

producer (prə dü′sər) a living thing that makes its own food (p. 95)

protein (prō′tēn) a substance that is used by organisms to build cells (p. 108)

protist (prō′tist) a one-celled living thing with a nucleus and other cell parts (p. 106)

quartz (kwôrts) a common rock-forming mineral with large crystals that can be many different colors (p. 197)

radiolarian (rā′ dē ō ler′ ē ən) an animal-like protist that has an outer skeleton; plural radiolaria (p. 106)

rain forest (rān′fôr′ist) an ecosystem that has large amounts of precipitation and thick plant growth (p. 130)

recycle (rē sī′ kəl) use materials again (p. 105)

remains (ri māns′) what is left of a dead organism (p. 96)

repel (ri pel′) to be pulled away from each other (p. 9)

resistance (ri zis′təns) property of a material that does not allow electric current to flow easily through it (p. 15)

resistor (ri zis′tər) a material that does not allow electric charges to flow easily (p. 15)

resource (ri sôrs′) a material that meets the need of a living thing (p. 103)

river (riv′ər) a large stream of water that flows into a lake or an ocean (p. 238)

rock cycle (rok sī′kəl) the process that recycles rock into new types of rock (p. 214)

rotor (rō′tər) the electromagnet part of a motor, sometimes called the armature (p. 62)

salt marsh (sȯlt märsh) an area of land that is covered by saltwater for part of the year (p. 156)

sand dune (sand dün) a landform similar to a hill made of sand (p. 244)

scavenger (skav′ən jər) an organism that feeds on dead or decaying plants and animals (p. 96)

scientific method (sī′ən tif′ik meth′əd) organized ways of finding answers and solving problems (p. 76)

EM12

secondary consumer (sek′ən der′ē kən sü′mər) an animal that eats the primary consumer in a food chain (p. 99)

sediment (sed′ə mənt) any earth material that has been moved from one place to another and laid down on the surface of Earth (p. 210)

sedimentary (sed′ə men′tər ē) type of rock that forms when layers of sediments settle on top of one another and harden (p. 210)

seed dispersal (sēd dis pėr′səl) the process of scattering plant seeds (p. 166)

seedling (sēd′ling) a young plant (p. 151)

sequence (sē′kwəns) the order in which things happen (p. 231)

series circuit (sir′ēz sėr′kit) a circuit in which electric charge can flow only in one path (p. 16)

short circuit (shôrt sėr′kit) electric current that follows a path other than the path meant for its flow (p. 24)

shrub (shrub) a woody plant that does not have a single trunk like a tree (p. 128)

silt (silt) very fine pieces of soil (p. 239)

soil (soil) the thin layer of loose, weathered material that covers most of the land surface of Earth (p. 239)

stamen (stā′mən) the male structure in plants (p. 164)

static electricity (stat′ik i lek′tris′ə tē) the build-up of positive or negative electric charges (p. 9)

streak (strēk) the color of the powder that a mineral leaves when it is scratched across a special plate (p. 199)

survive (sər vīv′) stay alive (p. 95)

swamp (swämp) a type of wetland where trees can grow (p. 127)

symbiosis (sim′bē ō′ sis) a relationship between two organisms that helps one or both of the organisms (p. 132)

temperate (tem′pər it) neither too hot nor too cold (p. 131)

temperature (tem′pər ə chər) a measure of how hot or cold something is (p. 125)

territory (ter′ə tôr′ē) an area where an animal lives, and which it defends from others (p. 154)

trait (trāt) a feature an organism gets from its parents (p. 156)

transport (tran spôrt′) to carry from one place to another (p. 242)

tundra (tun′ drə) a cold and dry ecosystem where the ground is frozen all year long (p. 127)

turbine (tėr′bən) a machine that is turned by the power of wind or water (p. 64)

understory (un′dər stôr′ē) the area of a rain forest below the canopy (p. 130)

valley (val′ē) the low land between two mountains (p. 233)

vent (vent) an opening in a volcano (p. 248)

volcano (vol kā′nō) place on Earth's crust where magma reaches the surface (p. 248)

waste (wāst) the unused or leftover parts (p. 96)

weathering (weŦH′ər ing) the process that breaks down rocks in Earth's crust into smaller pieces (p. 234)

wetland (wet′land′) place where the ground is covered with water for at least part of the year (p. 127)

Index

This index lists the pages on which topics appear in this book. Page numbers after a *p* refer to a photograph or drawing. Page numbers after a *c* refer to a chart, graph, or diagram.

Credits

Illustrations

9-10, 12, 14, 16, 18, 20, 22, 24 Big Sesh Studios; 16, 23, 39, 46-47 Peter Bollinger; 39, 65, 125 Tony Randazzo; 104, 233-234, 236, 240, 242, 244, 246, 248, 250-251 Adam Benton; 126 Robert Kayganich; 157, 216-217 Jeff Mangiat; 165 Robert Ulrich; 228 Alan Male

Photographs

Every effort has been made to secure permission and provide appropriate credit for photographic material. The publisher deeply regrets any omission and pledges to correct errors called to its attention in subsequent editions.

Unless otherwise acknowledged, all photographs are the property of Scott Foresman, a division of Pearson Education.

Photo locators denoted as follows: Top (T), Center (C), Bottom (B), Left (L), Right (R), Background (Bkgd).

Cover: (L) ©Gary Bell/zefa/Corbis, (C) ©Royalty-Free/Corbis

Front Matter: ii ©DK Images; iii ©Royalty-Free/Corbis; v Jerry Young/©DK Images; vi (TL) ©Cameron/Corbis, (TL) ©Jan Stromme/Getty Images; vii (B) ©GK & Vikki Hart/Getty Images, (B) ©Georgette Douwma/Getty Images, (TR) ©Johnny Johnson/Getty Images, (T) ©Jeremy Walker/Photo Researchers, Inc.; viii (BL) ©Breck P. Kent/Animals Animals/Earth Scenes, (TL) ©George D. Lepp/Corbis, (T) Getty Images; ix (B) ©Chris Mattison/Frank Lane Picture Agency/Corbis, (CR) ©Orion Press/Corbis, (T) ©Phyllis Greenberg/Animals Animals/Earth Scenes; x (B) ©W. Cody/Corbis, (T) Courtesy of Lisa Boulton/California Cavern; xi (T) ©Soames Summerhays/Photo Researchers, Inc., (B) ©Susan Rayfield/Photo Researchers, Inc., (TR) ©Ted Mead/PhotoLibrary; xii Creatas; xiii ©John A. L. Cooke/Animals Animals/Earth Scenes; xiv ©Peter Gridley/Getty Images; xv ©David Welling/Nature Picture Library

Unit A – Opener: 1 ©David Wall/Alamy Images; 2 (Bkgd) ©Phillip James Corwin/Corbis, (CR) ©Robert Holmes/Corbis; 3 ©Jan Stromme/Getty Images; 4 ©Byron Aughenbaugh/Getty Images; 5 ©DK Images; 7 ©Byron Aughenbaugh/Getty Images; 8 ©Byron Aughenbaugh/Getty Images; 12 ©DK Images; 14 ©DK Images; 15 (BR) ©Richard Hamilton smith/Corbis, (CL) ©Richard Megna/Fundamental Photographs; 16 ©DK Images; 17 ©DK Images; 18 (B) ©Amy Trustram Eve/Photo Researchers, Inc., (CR) ©Andrew Syred/Photo Researchers, Inc.; 19 (TR) ©Jeff Greenberg/Index Stock Imagery, (CR) ©Reuters NewMedia Inc./Corbis, (BR) ©Mark C. Burnett/Photo Researchers, Inc.; 20 ©DK Images; 24 Corbis; 25 ©Tony Freeman/PhotoEdit; 26 AGE Fotostock; 30 (Bkgd) Getty Images, (TL) ©Byron Aughenbaugh/Getty Images; 34 (Bkgd) Corbis, (CL) Jupiter Images, (BR) Getty Images; 35 (TL, BL) Getty Images; 36 (R)©Jose Luis Pelaez, Inc./Corbis, (CR) ©wwwblende11de/Getty Images; 37 ©Johnny Johnson/Getty Images; 38 ©Jeremy Walker/Photo Researchers, Inc.; 39 ©Cordelia Molloy/Photo Researchers, Inc.; 41 (Bkgd) ©Tibor Bognar/Corbis, (R) ©Stevie Grand/Photo Researchers, Inc.; 42 ©Martin Bond/Photo Researchers, Inc.; 43 ©Martin Bond/Photo Researchers, Inc.; 44 ©Cordelia Molloy/Photo Researchers, Inc.; 46 ©Timothy Hearsum/Getty Images; 47 (TR, CR, BR) ©Loren Winters/Visuals Unlimited; 48 (TL, BR) ©DK Images; 50 Andy Crawford/©DK Images; 54 (B, BR) Andy Crawford/©DK Images; 58 (C) Used with permission of GE Healthcare., (BL) ©Sheila Terry/Photo Researchers, Inc., (TR) ©Richard Megna/Fundamental Photographs, (TL) ©Jeremy Walker/Photo Researchers, Inc.; 59 ©Jeremy Walker/Photo Researchers, Inc.; 60 Dave King/Courtesy of The Science Museum, London/©DK Images; 61 (TR) Dave King/Courtesy of The Science Museum, London/©DK Images, (C) Clive Streeter/Courtesy of The Science Museum, London/©DK Images; 62 (B, TL) ©GK & Vikki Hart/Getty Images; 64 (C) ©Philip James Corwin/Corbis, (TL) Getty Images; 70 (Bkgd) ©Kevin Schafer/Getty Images, (TL) ©Martin Bond/Photo Researchers, Inc., (CL) Andy Crawford/©DK Images, (BL) ©DK Images; 74 (T) The Granger Collection, NY, (L) Getty Images, (BL) AGE Fotostock; 75 (TL) ©Jan Stromme/Getty Images, (CL) ©Johnny Johnson/Getty Images, (B) ©Robert Holmes/Corbis; 81 ©Stockdisc/Getty Images; 82 ©Blow Up/Getty Images; **Unit B – Opener:** 87 (Bkgd) ©Richard Price/Getty Images, (CR) ©Larry Minden/Minden Pictures; 88 ©Thomas Hallstein/Ambient Images, Inc.; 89 ©George D. Lepp/Corbis; 90 (Bkgd) ©David Muench/Corbis, (BL) ©John Gerlach/Animals Animals/Earth Scenes, (BC) ©George H. H. Huey/Corbis, (BR) ©Joe McDonald/Corbis; 91 (B, TR, BR) Getty Images, (TCR, BR) ©DK Images, (BCR) ©Andrew Syred/Photo Researchers, Inc., (BL, BC) Corbis, (BCL) ©Naturfoto Honal/Corbis, (BC) ©Tom Brakefield/Corbis, (BR) ©John Shaw/Tom Stack & Associates, Inc., (BC, B) Neil Fletcher and Matthew Ward/©DK Images, (BR) ©Michael Sewell/Peter Arnold, Inc., (BR) Jane Burton/©DK Images, (BR) ©Daniel Cox/Getty Images, (BR) ©Stephen J. Krasemann/DRK Photo; 93 ©George D. Lepp/Corbis; 94 ©David Muench/Corbis; 95 (BR) ©Roger Phillips/©DK Images, (TR) ©Royalty-Free/Corbis; 96 (B) ©John Cancalosi/Nature Picture Library, (TL) ©Tom Brakefield/Corbis; 97 (R) ©Zig Leszczynski/Animals Animals/Earth Scenes, (TR) ©Frank Lane Picture Agency/Corbis, (CR) ©Joe McDonald/Corbis, (TL) ©John Gerlach/Animals Animals/Earth Scenes, (TC) ©Tim Fitzharris/Minden Pictures, (BL) ©George H. H. Huey/Corbis, (CL) ©Darren Bennett/Animals Animals/Earth Scenes, (BR) ©DK Images; 98 (BR) ©Naturfoto Honal/Corbis, (CL) Corbis, (TL) Getty Images; 99 ©Tom Brakefield/Corbis; 100 (BCL) Neil Fletcher and Matthew Ward/©DK Images, (BR) Jane Burton/©DK Images, (CC) ©John Shaw/Tom Stack & Associates, Inc., (CR) ©Michael Quinton/Minden Pictures, (BC) ©DK Images, (TCL) Corbis, (TL) Getty Images; 101 (TR) ©Michael Sewell/Peter Arnold, Inc., (CL) Getty Images, (T) ©Daniel Cox/Getty Images; 102 (L) ©Sally A. Morgan/Corbis, (BR) ©DK Images; 103 ©Raymond Gehman/Corbis; 104 ©DK Images; 106 (BC) ©Alfred Pasieka/Photo Researchers, Inc., (BR, BCR) ©Steve Gschmeissner/Photo Researchers, Inc., (TL) ©Biophoto Associates/Photo Researchers, Inc., (B) ©Robert George Young/Masterfile Corporation; 107 (BL, CR) ©Andrew Syred/Photo Researchers, Inc., (TL) Getty Images, (CR) ©Microfield Scientific Ltd./Photo Researchers, Inc., (TCR) ©SciMAT/Photo Researchers, Inc.; 108 (BL) ©Sinclair Stammers/Photo Researchers, Inc., (C) Clive Streeter/©DK Images, (TCR) ©Tony Craddock/Photo Researchers, Inc., (TL) ©Jerry Young/©DK Images; 109 (CL) ©Andrew Syred/Photo Researchers, Inc., (C) ©Dr. David Patterson/Photo Researchers, Inc., (CR) ©Eric Grave/Photo Researchers, Inc.; 110 (Bkgd) ©Steve Allen/Getty Images, (BC) ©Alain Choisnet/Getty Images; 114 (CL) Corbis, (CL) Getty Images, (CL) ©Naturfoto Honal/Corbis, (CL) ©Tom Brakefield/Corbis, (Bkgd) ©Pat O'Hara/Corbis, (TL) ©David Muench/Corbis, (CL) ©Sally A. Morgan/Corbis, (BL) ©Alfred Pasieka/Photo Researchers, Inc., (BR) ©Andrew Syred/Photo Researchers, Inc.; 116 Getty Images; 118 (BR) ©Alan G. Nelson/Animals Animals/Earth Scenes, (BL) ©Tom Edwards/Animals Animals/Earth Scenes, (CL) ©George Rinhart/Corbis; 119 ©Breck P. Kent/Animals Animals/Earth Scenes; 120 (T) Hauser/laif/©Aurora Photos, (B) ©George Ranalli/Photo Researchers, Inc.; 121 (BL) ©Georgette Douwma/Getty Images, (BR) Jane Burton/©DK Images; 123 (CR) ©DK Images, (Bkgd) ©Larry Michael/Nature Picture Library; 124 ©Andrew Brown/Ecoscene/Corbis; 126 (BL, TL) ©David Keaton/Corbis, (BCL) ©Aaron Horowitz/Corbis, 127 (TR) ©Michael Townsend/Getty Images, (CR) ©David Samuel Robbins/Corbis; 128 (TL) ©Andrew Brown/Ecoscene/Corbis, (B) ©George Ranalli/Photo Researchers, Inc.; 129 ©Hans Strand/Corbis; 130 (T) ©Royalty-Free/Corbis, (Bkgd) Hauser/laif/©Aurora Photos; 131 (TR) ©Tim Fitzharris/Minden Pictures, (BC) ©DK Images; 132 (BL) ©Jane Burton/©DK Images, (BR) ©Dave King/©DK Images, (TL) ©Georgette Douwma/Getty Images; 133 ©Georgette Douwma/Getty Images; 134 ©Alan Kearney/Getty Images; 138 (Bkgd) ©Jan Tove Johansson/Getty Images, (B) ©Hauser/laif/©Aurora Photos, (TL) ©Hans Strand/Corbis, (TL) ©Andrew Brown/Ecoscene/Corbis; 140 ©DK Images; 142 ©Roger Ressmeyer/Corbis; 144 (Bkgd) ©Ralph White/Corbis, (TR) NOAA; 145 ©Orion Press/Corbis; 146 (B) ©Steve Kaufman/Corbis, (BR) ©Joe McDonald/Animals Animals/Earth Scenes, (Bkgd) ©Larry Michael/Nature Picture Library, (CL, CR) ©D. Robert & Lorri Franz/Corbis; 147 (BL) ©W. Treat Davidson/Photo Researchers, Inc., (T) ©George D. Lepp/Corbis, (CR) ©Tim Davis/Corbis, (BR) ©DK Images; 149 ©Orion Press/Corbis; 150 ©Ron Austing/Frank Lane Picture Agency/Corbis; 151 (TR) ©DK Images, (BR) ©Frank BlackburnEcoscene/Corbis; 152 (BR) ©Bill Curtsinger/NGS Image Collection, (CL) ©L. Rue/Corbis, (TL) ©DK Images; 153 ©T. Kitchin & V. Hurst/NHPA Limited; 154 (TR) ©George D. Lepp/Corbis, (BL) ©Joe McDonald/Corbis, (TL) ©DK Images; 155 (BR) ©Nigel Bean/Nature Picture Library, (TR) ©Karl Switak/NHPA Limited; 156 (BL, CL) ©Ray Richardson/Animals Animals/Earth Scenes, (TL) ©DK Images; 157 ©Tim Davis/Corbis; 158 (CL) ©Hal Horwitz/Corbis, (BL) ©Jack Wilburn/Animals Animals/Earth Scenes, (BR) ©Tony Wharton/Frank Lane Picture Agency/Corbis, (TR) ©Galen Rowell/Corbis, (TL) ©DK Images; 159 (BL) ©TH-Foto/zefa/Corbis, (BR) ©Chris Mattison/Frank Lane Picture Agency/Corbis, (TR) ©Peter/Georgina Bowater/Mira; 160 (BR) ©Jerry Young/©DK Images, (BL) ©Michael & Patricia Fogden/Minden Pictures, (CL) ©Rod Planck/Photo Researchers, Inc., (CL) ©Frans Lanting/Minden Pictures; 161 (CR) ©Darrell Gulin/Corbis, (TR) Getty Images; 162 (TL) ©DK Images, (C) ©Konrad Wothe/Minden Pictures; 163 (BR) ©Phyllis Greenberg/Animals Animals/Earth Scenes, (BR) ©Karen Tweedy-Holmes/Corbis, (TC) ©Derek Hall/©DK Images, (TL) ©Aaron Haupt/Photo Researchers, Inc., (CR) Sue Atkinson/©DK Images; 164 (BR, TL) ©Merlin Tuttle/BCI/Photo Researchers, Inc., (TR) ©W. Treat Davidson/Photo Researchers, Inc.; 166 (TR) ©George D. Lepp/Corbis, (BR, TL) ©DK Images, (BL) ©Herbert Kehrer/zefa/Corbis; 167 (TL) ©DK Images, (BR) ©Andrew McRobb/©DK Images, (TC) ©Tobias Bernhard/zefa/Corbis, (TL) Stephen Oliver/©DK Images; 168 ©Chris Newbert/Minden Pictures; 172 (Bkgd, CL) Getty Images, (BR) ©Herbert Kehrer/zefa/Corbis, (TL) ©Ron Austing/Frank Lane Picture Agency/Corbis, (BL) ©W. Treat Davidson/Photo Researchers, Inc., (TL) ©Tim Davis/Corbis; 176 (Bkgd) ©Neale Clark/Robert Harding Picture Library Ltd., (TL) NASA; 177 (TL) ©George D. Lepp/Corbis, (BL) ©Thomas Hallstein/Ambient Images, Inc., (CL) ©Breck P. Kent/Animals Animals/Earth Scenes, (CL) ©Orion Press/Corbis; 182 (C) ©Dorling Kindersley/Getty Images, (C) ©Taxi/Getty Images; 184 (BR) ©Leroy Simon/Getty Images, (B) Jerry Young/©DK Images; **Unit C – Opener:** 189 (Bkgd) ©Pat O'Hara/Getty Images, (T) ©William Whitehurst/Corbis; 190 (Bkgd) ©Phillip Schermeister/Getty Images, (CR) ©John Elk III/Ambient Images, Inc.; 191 ©Kevin Schafer/Getty Images; 192 (BR) ©Colin Keates/Courtesy of the Natural History Museum, London/©DK Images, (T) Courtesy of Lisa Boulton/California Cavern; 192 ©DK Images; 193 (TR) Colin Keates/Courtesy of the Natural History Museum, London/©DK Images, (BR) Natural History Museum, London/©DK Images, (BCR) Royal Museum of Scotland/©DK Images, (T, BR, TR) ©DK Images; 195 (Bkgd) Courtesy of Lisa Boulton/California Cavern, (CR) Getty Images; 196 Courtesy of Lisa Boulton/California Cavern; 197 (TCR, TR, BCR) ©DK Images, (BR) ©Dr. Rich Busch/Earth Science World Image Bank/American Geological Institute; 198 (TC, C) ©Earth Science World Image Bank/American Geological Institute, (TL) ©E. R. Degginger/Color-Pic, Inc., (CC) Colin Keates/Courtesy of the Natural History Museum, London/©DK Images, (TCL) Harry Taylor/©DK Images, (BL, CL, BR) ©DK Images; 199 (CC, CL, BR, CR, C, TR) ©DK Images, (TR, BCR) Colin Keates/The Natural History Museum, London/©DK Images; 200 (BL) Natural History Museum/©DK Images, (CR) ©DK Images, (TC) Colin Keates/Courtesy of the Natural History Museum, London/©DK Images, (CR) ©Breck P. Kent Natural History Photography, (TR) ©Jeff Scovil, (BR) ©M. Claye/Jacana Scientific Control/Photo Researchers, Inc.; 201 (T) ©DK Images, (CR) ©Breck P. Kent/Animals Animals/Earth Scenes, (BR) ©Carey B. Van Loon; 202 (TL, C) ©DK Images, (BL) ©Phil Degginger/Getty Images; 203 (TL) Colin Keates/Courtesy of the Natural History Museum, London/©DK Images, (BR) Judith Miller/Freeman's/©DK Images; 204 (TL) ©DK Images, (TR) Colin Keates/Courtesy of the Natural History Museum, London/©DK Images, (BR) ©Royalty-Free/Corbis; 205 (BR) ©John Anderson/Animals Animals/Earth Scenes, (TR) ©Lester Lefkowitz/Corbis, (CR) Jupiter Images; 206 ©DK Images; 207 (TL, CR) ©Harry Taylor/©DK Images, (CL) ©Dr. Marli Miller/Visuals Unlimited, (BCL, BL) ©DK Images, (BCR) ©Ross Frid/Visuals Unlimited, (TR) Colin Keates/Courtesy of the Natural History Museum, London/©DK Images; 208 (BL, TL) ©DK Images, (CL) Natural History Museum, London/©DK Images; 209 (TC, TR) ©DK Images, (TL) Colin Keates/Courtesy of the Natural History Museum, London/©DK Images, (TR) ©DK Images, (BR) ©Jerome Wyckoff/Animals Animals/Earth Scenes; 210 (T) ©Astrid & Hans-Frieder Michler/SPL/Photo Researchers, Inc., (B) ©James J. Stachecki/Animals Animals/Earth Scenes; 211 (BR) ©Dr. Marli Miller/Visuals Unlimited, (TCL, BR) ©DK Images, (BCR) Dave King/©DK Images; 212 (TL) Richard M. Busch, (B) ©Gregory G. Dimijian, M.D./Photo Researchers, Inc.; 213 (TC, TL) ©DK Images, (TR) Richard M. Busch; 214 (C) ©DK Images, (B) ©Andrew J. Martinez/Photo Researchers, Inc.; 215 (T, C, BCC) ©DK Images; 218 ©Anthony Bannister/Gallo Images/Corbis; 219 ©Albert J. Copley/Visuals Unlimited, ©Ken Lucas/Visuals Unlimited, ©Mark Schneider/Visuals Unlimited, ©William Weber/Visuals Unlimited, ©Carolina Biological/Visuals Unlimited; 222 ©Dr.

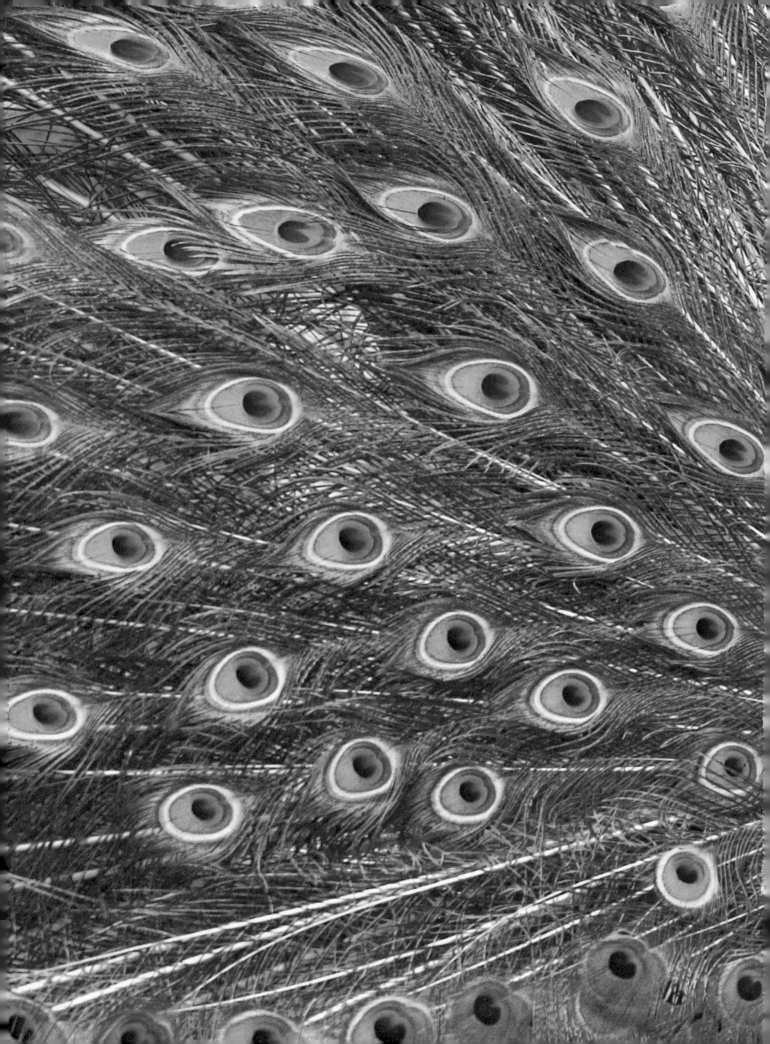